Digital Nomads Living on the Margins

EMERALD STUDIES IN ALTERNATIVITY AND MARGINALIZATION

Series Editors:
Samantha Holland, Leeds Beckett University, UK, and Karl Spracklen, Leeds Beckett University, UK

There is growing interest in work on transgression, liminality, and subcultural capital within cultural studies, sociology, and the social sciences more broadly. However, there is a lack of understanding of the problem of alternativity: what it means to be alternative in culture and society in modernity. What "alternative" looks like is often left unexplored. The alternative is either assumed un-problematically or stands in for some other form of social and cultural exclusion.

Alternativity delineates those spaces, scenes, subcultures, objects, and practices in modern society that are actively designed to be counter or resistive to mainstream popular culture. Alternativity is associated with marginalization, both actively pursued by individuals and imposed on individuals and subcultures. Alternativity was originally represented and constructed through acts of transgression and through shared subcultural capital. In contemporary society, alternative music scenes such as heavy metal, goth, and punk have spread around the world, and alternative fashions and embodiment practices are now adopted by footballers and fashion models. The nature of alternativity as a communicative lifeworld is now questioned in an age of globalization and hyper-commodification.

This book series provides a stimulus to new research and new theorizing on alternativity and marginalization. It provides a focus for scholars interested in sociological and cultural research that expands our understanding of the ontological status of spaces, scenes, subcultures, objects, and practices defined as alternative, liminal, or transgressive. In turn, the book series enables scholars to theorize about the status of the alternative in contemporary culture and society.

Titles in this series

Amanda DiGioia, *Childbirth and Parenting in Horror Texts: The Marginalized and the Monstrous.*

Karl Spracklen and Beverley Spracklen, *The Evolution of Goth Culture: The Origins and Deeds of the New Goths.*

Samantha Holland and Karl Spracklen (Eds), *Subcultures, Bodies and Spaces: Essays on Alternativity and Marginalization.*

Stephen Brown and Marie-Cécile Cervellon, *Revolutionary Nostalgia: Neo-Burlesque, Retromania and Social Change.*

Asya Draganova, *Popular Music in Contemporary Bulgaria: At the Crossroads.*

Eleanor Peters, *The Use and Abuse of Music: Criminal Records.*

Digital Nomads Living on the Margins: Remote-Working Laptop Entrepreneurs in the Gig Economy

BY

BEVERLY YUEN THOMPSON
Siena College, USA

emerald PUBLISHING

United Kingdom – North America – Japan – India – Malaysia – China

Emerald Publishing Limited
Howard House, Wagon Lane, Bingley BD16 1WA, UK

First edition 2021

British Library Cataloguing in Publication Data
A catalogue record for this book is available from the British Library

ISBN: 978-1-80071-546-2 (Print)
ISBN: 978-1-80071-545-5 (Online)
ISBN: 978-1-80071-547-9 (Epub)

Printed and bound by CPI Group (UK) Ltd, Croydon, CR0 4YY

ISOQAR REGISTERED
Certificate Number 1985
ISO 14001

ISOQAR certified Management System, awarded to Emerald for adherence to Environmental standard ISO 14001:2004.

INVESTOR IN PEOPLE

Dedicated to Margaret Kwei-On Yuen and Robert G. Thompson.
Dedicated to all struggling workers in the gig economy.

Contents

Contents

About the Author

Beverly Yuen Thompson is an Associate Professor of Sociology at Siena College, Loudonville, New York. She is the author of *Covered in Ink: Tattoos, Women and the Politics of the Body* (2015, NYU Press), an ethnography of heavily tattooed women and female tattoo artists in the United States. She has published on the topic of gender and marginalized subcultures.

Introduction

The Digital Nomad

Digital Nomads in Pandemic Times

I am writing during the coronavirus COVID-19 pandemic, which has significantly altered the context of the digital nomad lifestyle. Pandemics and environmental catastrophes will likely continue to have increasing impacts on both leisure travel and remote work in ways only currently speculated upon. Before the pandemic – digital nomads – or remote workers who use their freedom-from-location to travel the world – were an odd minority. I envision them as "canaries in the digital coalmine." They point to the vulnerabilities of future employment models for the next generations. Overnight as we entered the pandemic crisis, many white-collar workers were thrown into a digital workplace, as they were quarantined in their homes, along with family members, and children released from school. For the top tech workers, such as those at Google and Microsoft, they have the privilege of continuing their work from home for the indefinite future (C. Duffy, 2020). Of course, the top tech and start-up workers are best positioned for remote work. Twitter is allowing its staff to work from home "forever" (Baron, 2020). The pandemic brought to light the impact of decades of dismantling and underfunding social safety nets and health care, environmental racism, widespread inequalities, and high rates of poverty in the United States and beyond. As millions lose their employment in the United States, even more desperate workers will seek employment on digital freelance platforms, competing with the already struggling entry-level digital nomad workers. As more people work remotely, their ability to travel or move to new locations increases, potentially shifting urban density. Digital nomads often found their hometowns prohibitively expensive, and the ability to live abroad more cheaply was one motivating factor. Now that is true for even more people. Matthew Haag (2020) writes for the *New York Times* an article entitled, "Manhattan Faces a Reckoning If Working From Home Becomes the Norm," in which he points out that finance firms and other high-expense Manhattan employers may not only allow workers to telecommute, but they may shutter their offices altogether and save billions in rent. Haag writes,

**Digital Nomads Living on the Margins:
Remote-Working Laptop Entrepreneurs in the Gig Economy, 1–11**

**Published under exclusive licence by Emerald Publishing Limited
doi:10.1108/978-1-80071-545-520211001**

> Before the coronavirus crisis, three of New York City's largest commercial tenants – Barclays, JP Morgan Chase and Morgan Stanley – had tens of thousands of workers in towers across Manhattan. Now, as the city wrestles with when and how to reopen, executives at all three firms have decided that it is highly unlikely that all their workers will ever return to those buildings.

If such high-paid tech workers were released from their offices, why would they continue to live in New York City when they could be anywhere in the world? While the travel industry has been grounded and shuttered for the time being, the industry continues to offer incentives for customers, and the irresistibly low prices – and loss of jobs – will entice people to once again travel, and thus, digital nomadism may be set to expand in the post-pandemic future.

In this introductory chapter, I will consider the rise in popularity of the digital nomad concept. I will discuss the methodology used for empirical data collection on digital nomads. I then turn to a brief overview of each chapter. This book provides a critical examination of the digital nomad lifestyle, concept, and community and contextualizes it within a sociological perspective of neoliberal capitalism, the gig economy, and escalating global inequality.

Defining the Digital Nomad

At the dawn of the internet, Tsugio Makimoto and David Manners (1997) wrote their manifesto *Digital Nomad*. In this book, they speculated about the potential of the internet to liberate workers from the shackles of their office – they could use a computer to work and relocate somewhere pleasant and more affordable – like the beach! This image has been latched onto by a subculture – decades later – that have adopted Makimoto and Manner's term, "digital nomad," as they pose with laptops on the beach that the authors envisioned. The underlying orientation of Makimoto and Manners' (1997) *Digital Nomad* is that of freedom and serious travel. For example, Ina Reichenberger (2017) reflects the zeitgeist of popular nomadic lifestyle literature: "Freedom then appeared in a variety of contexts, including freedom within paid employment, freedom relating to location independence and freedom to pursue self-development" (p. 9). Indeed, one of the popular authors that digital nomads latch onto early in their subcultural career is Tim Ferriss's (2009) book *The 4-Hour Workweek*, which pledges to provide a blueprint on how to barely work and make more money than ever. "However," Muller (2016) cautions,

> the digital nomad should not be confused with the figure of a dropout. Although the dropout and the digital nomad share an interest in designing a self-determined life, the value of labor productivity is an important feature in the lifestyle of digital nomads. (p. 345)

Digital nomads are obsessed with their work and promoting their brand; indeed, it is of which they think while engaging in their leisure or dreaming of their future destinations. In Cook's (2020) findings, digital nomads struggle with disciplinary practices of balancing work and leisure, especially in tourist locations and when new to the lifestyle.

The nomads attempt to distinguish themselves from the more assumedly low-brow "tourist," on their cruise ships or package tours. Digital nomads like to think of themselves as "world-citizens," or "travelers," or indeed, nomads, freedom-seekers. At any rate, the attempt is one of achieving authenticity (Azariah, 2016). Yet, Wood (2005) argues, "the nomad and the global tourist are two aspects of the same process; their relationship to the world is primarily aesthetic" (p. 54). In Reichenberger's (2017) study of digital nomads, she states that the subculture created a hierarchy around one's commitment to travel. Those able to work remotely 100% of the time and travel continuously were at the pinnacle, those with less time or flexibility to travel to the furthest places, the most exotic, remote, and trendiest, followed. Yet, they too, live in co-living/coworking spaces, like tourists on a cruise ship, they rarely engage with the locals on a deeper level than all-inclusive resort vacationers. At any rate, while the pathways of the nomads and tourist do not diverge widely, the perception that nomads have of their lifestyle is that of the enlightened traveler, exchanging the consumer lifestyle of property ownership and material accumulation for one of travel and collection of mementos.

Methodology

This research adopts the methodology of ethnography and the aligned sociological theory of symbolic interaction, which Blumer (1969) describes as the "distinctive character of interaction as it takes place between human beings" (p. 79). Paul Atkinson, Delamont, and Housley (2008) takes the definition further:

> Things have social lives. They are produced, reproduced, and exchanged. They are the objects and outcomes of socially organized work, and they are embedded in networks of social relations. They are endowed with meaning. They are collected and displayed. They permit social activity and they also constrain social action. Material goods and objects are thoroughly social, and they are a fundamental part of cultural life .... They are used to enact memory, to express individual biography, and to enshrine collective identity. (p. 119)

Qualitative research centers the individual, and their perspective, in an attempt to understand how they make meaning of their social environment, and how their interactions reinforce these meanings, through actions and patterned behaviors. Social action and interaction reflect the larger social structures, institutions, and cultural norms (Blumer, 1969). Other terms are used to describe qualitative research process that also relate to this study. A phenomenological study approaches a particular phenomenon, an experience that applies to a group of people, and so by examining how the group has experienced a phenomenon, we can better understand that particular social ritual (i.e., grief and insomnia)

(Creswell, 2007). Similarly, Harold Garfinkel (1967) uses the term ethnomethodological to explain how researchers analyze everyday activities. Gleeson and Erben (1976) further describe the same concept as how members "directly experience the world and in the consequent effect this has on their intentionality and the consequent effect their intentionality has on the procedures of the world" (p. 477). They state that this can help researchers understand how people define their position within this particular social world and thus how they understand their "parameters and avenues for choice within the contexts of their defined everyday existence" (p. 482).

Overall, qualitative research methods – ethnography – can contribute a deeper understanding of how individuals make sense of their social world outside of the statistical numerical context of quantitative methods (Gibson-Graham, 2014). Denzin (2006) argues that conducting ethnography is also not an innocent practice but is political, performative, and pedagogical – we ultimately present the data (our participants experiences) – to an audience and thus we exercise some power over representation as researchers. Because ethnography is an interpersonal research method, in contrast to statistics methods where a researcher may never encounter the participants, the researcher themselves become a part of the data collection experience. Especially considering the ways in which the symbolic interaction perspective points to the significance of the micro-interactions of daily life and how these patterned behaviors reinforce larger institutional forces of power dynamics. Therefore, the interaction between that of researcher and participants can be one of a power dynamic; one in which an authority figure takes an individual's personal story, biological sample (in the case of medicine), or other personal data, for an abstract purpose.

After gaining Institutional Review Board (IRB) approval to being seeking participants, researchers confront the daunting task of finding their initial participants. If the researcher is studying a subculture in which they are already involved, they may already know the "cast of characters" (Lofland & Lofland, 1995, p. 37). For example, Mwenda Ntarangwi (2010) writes an ethnography from both an insider/outsider perspective, as an African anthropologist using field methods to observe the professional world of American anthropology, as enacted in the academy and professional conferences. Thus, he calls his study "reversed gaze," using the tools of anthropologists to study the hidden backstage of professional anthropologists as they work in universities, present at conferences, conduct fieldwork in foreign nations, and write about "the other" for a primarily Western audience. He feels this is important as it contributes "an African perspective into understanding anthropology" and to "decipher the underlying anthropological culture that has so much impacted the ways that Africans are studied and perceived" (Ntarangwi, 2010, p. 3).

Ethnographers often feel a responsibility toward their participants and want to be open about expressing their intentions and approaches to the subject matter – in short, they want to create a meaningful relationship between themselves and their participants (Pelias, 2009). As an insider, one might stress their commitment to the community. They will at any rate anticipate such questions from participants or might use their own experience as an opening to discuss similar experiences from the participants (Friedman, 1990, p. 64). Feminist theorists have also brought to the forefront the importance of assessing the embodied nature of research – as researchers we have a particular identity and embodiment that affects the interaction with participants, if we are like them or distinct, the emotional labor engaged in during ethnography, and the ways in which we talk about and experience our own bodies (Atkinson et al., 2008, p. 141).

Since we cannot interview or access all the individuals and data related to a particular topic, we must gather a sub-selection of participants that can represent the larger social issue, enough to gain a saturation of sampling representing most of the outcomes, and enough information to be generalizable to the class as a whole (Becker, 1998, p. 67). Finding participants is one of the first challenges researchers encounter – finding people that represent the issue at hand. These initial contacts are significant in the direction that they will lead the researcher to other contacts, which may reveal over time the political nature of the sub-community and the social pathways created by interpersonal politics (Duneier, 2011, p. 3). Researchers may need to find a particular organization, community center, or other specific locations in which their target population resides.

For this research on digital nomads, I first sought out online communities where nomads gather, to discuss the intricacies of their lifestyle, and to connect with other members with whom they can relate, share resources, and make friends. After exploring the online communities of digital nomads, I then personally attended three different digital nomad conferences in Europe in 2017. From these conferences, I was able to make contact with many digital nomads and complete 38 in-depth interviews. The first conference was an event targeted to digital nomads and newcomers, it was one of the first major conferences, originating in the German-speaking world and later branching into English. This took place in September 2017, in Lisbon, Portugal. The attendees were primarily white European and American millennials. All of the associated meetups took place in bars around the city, thus contributing a youth-oriented party atmosphere. While I soaked up the atmosphere at this conference, I did not interview participants from it.

The next two conferences were more in-depth experiences transpiring over a week and a half each. One was a digital nomad women's retreat in Spain (which I will simply refer to in this book as "the women's retreat," or more simply, "the retreat"). In this small seaside town, 15 women lived together in a co-living space for 10 days. In this immersive environment, I was able to spend a great deal of time with all of the participants. I was able to conduct many interviews during the retreat itself, as we would find a quiet area to speak about their experiences as female digital nomads. Subsequently, the founder passed my name to her colleagues and co-founders of another digital nomad conference event forthcoming. Their event was only a few weeks later, also in Spain, and they employed me as their photographer. The founders of this particular conference (which I will simple refer to as "the conference" in this book) aimed to promote women and people of color within the subculture. This was their second annual event, with their inaugural year launching in Thailand. During this particular September, protests for an independent Catalonia were transpiring, with an independence vote, a general strike, and daily protests providing the urban context. While I was in the streets photographing this social movement, I was struck by the lack of political interest among the digital nomads, who stayed within their coworking spaces and continued building their brand, ignoring the cheering crowds outside. Working closely with the co-organizers of the conference and attending most of the events in my capacity as photographer gave me excellent access to the community, with whom I developed a comradery (Creswell, 2007; Madison, 2020). For the next several months following the conference, I continued to interview most of the participants on Skype, as we found ourselves in different countries around the world.

Participant Demographics

In this section, I will briefly overview the main demographic categories of the 38 participants interviewed for this study.

Gender. There were 33 women and 5 men.

Citizenship. Seventeen interviewees were American. Six people were from the UK. There was one Austrian, two Australians, and six Canadians. Two individuals had backgrounds and passports from both Central America and Spain. One participant was from Nigeria and migrated to Ireland as a youth. Another participant was from the Netherlands. One interviewee was from Poland.

Languages. Twenty-two of the participants spoke only English. Sixteen spoke additional languages, primarily based on their own cultural background, as few participants learned a non-native tongue.

Age. Twelve of the participants were in their 20s. Twenty-two participants were in their 30s. Four participants were in their 40s. None of the participants were over the age of 49.

Race/ethnicity. Twenty-five participants were white. Five were black American or African or Afro-Caribbean. One was Indian and one was Chinese. Three were mixed-race with white and Asian or Pakistani backgrounds. Two were Hispanic white. One was Arab American.

Sexuality. Thirty participants identified as straight. Five identified as lesbian, queer, or gay. Three identified as bisexual or fluid.

Education. Twenty-three participants had a bachelor's degree. Six had a master's degree. One had a Juris Doctor or law degree. Two participants had PhDs. One had an associate degree. Three had some college. One was in college. And one had only attended high school. Nineteen of the participants did not have student loan debt. Eighteen of the participants did have student loan debt, especially the Americans, and the British were the next worse off with high debts. Those from the UK and Australia only paid a small tax – if they had an income – for their repayment and did not need to pay if they had little to no income. Four participants were in deferment. The highest debt amount was $130,000.

Marital status. Thirty-two participants were single or not married. Ten of them were in relationships. Six participants were married; but of those, two were getting divorced.

Children. Thirty-seven of the participants did not have children. The one with children was now retired, and the children were grown adults. None of the interviewees were currently raising children. Did they want children in the future? Six said yes, two qualified their statements. Fifteen were unsure, ambivalent, or pushed the idea far into the future. Fourteen were quite confident that they did not want children.

Criminal record. Thirty-seven participants did not disclose any criminal record. One had previously been convicted of a "driving under the influence" charge, but it had since been expunged. Having a criminal record can impact one's ability to travel, as many countries ask about such records. This is rarely discussed among digital nomads and travelers but does impact millions of people globally.

Religion. Of 14 participants who mentioned religion, only two identified with an established religion: They were Christian and Muslim.

Property owner. Of the 10 participants who mentioned property ownership, four were current homeowners.

Book Overview

Chapter 1. Digital Nomads, Liquid Modernity, and the COVID-19 Pandemic

In the first chapter, we place the digital nomad concept within the theories of "liquid times," by Zygmunt Bauman (2000), this era marked by uncertainty, diminishing government, rising corporate rule, and shifting individual allegiances. (Nationalist) "community" belongs to the solidity of the past, which Bauman (2000) calls

> the last relic of the old-time utopias of the good society; it stands for whatever has been left of the dreams of a better life shared with better neighbors all following better rules of cohabitation. (p. 92)

Bauman describes this community as an idealized "short-cut to togetherness," a grouping of people with sheer, comforting sameness (p. 99). He also labels these moments of collective sameness as "carnival communities" or "explosive communities are events breaking the monotony of daily solitude" (p. 99). These concepts capture both the larger economic context of hyper-capitalism in which digital nomads are embedded and their subcultural gatherings at conferences and co-living spaces where they re-inscribe what it means to be a member of this community. This capitalist instability is one more element of the naturally disoriented nature of nomadic life. The digital nomad is adapted for "the crisis of late capitalist society engaged in a long-term historical process of destroying jobs security, while the virtues of work are ironically and ever more insistently being glorified" (Aronowitz et al., 1998, p. 40). Impoverishment is no longer only for the poor, as middle- and upper-income workers feel the squeeze of the new-order of downsizing, shrinking labor union protection, loss of state welfare, and (job-replacing) technologies (Aronowitz, Esposito, DiFazio, & Yard, 1998). In this world, long-term employment with a family wage and benefits is dissolved. Makimoto and Manners (1997) specified workers in web design and computer information would be the most likely to be remote workers. Using the framework of Doyle and Conboy's (2020) theoretical application of a liquid-modern perspective to the COVID-19 pandemic, the final section examines how the pandemic provides a liquid event furthering the social instabilities. This chapter focuses on theories of the neoliberal economy and the creation of the "gig economy" through the loss of "good jobs" in order to contextualize the plight of millennial age digital nomads as they employ the rhetoric of "freedom" while riding a wave of ultimate downward mobility. The COVID-19 pandemic has only increased such instabilities and exasperated such inequalities, especially those related to technological and platform employment.

Chapter 2. Western Millennials: Demographics and Socioeconomic Status

In this chapter, digital nomads are positioned within the socioeconomic context of millennials in Western countries, by examining some data and theories of generation-cohort outcomes. Moos, Pfeiffer, and Vinodrai (2018) address how the millennial demographic should be taken into account in regard to policy and urban planning as they represent major behavioral shifts in lifestyle and demographics. Millennials are the most highly educated generation in the United States at 38% (Fry, 2018, p. 54). This chapter will explore this demographic and socioeconomic context of the digital nomad participants interviewed for this book. This chapter will look at the background of the participants including factors, such as family wealth, social class, nationality, education, debt/asset, gender and sexual orientation, political engagement and workforce participation. From this overview, we can understand the general background of digital nomads and how the lifestyle may be unobtainable for others. Finally, this chapter contextualizes how the neoliberal national context and shrinking social safety net makes this lifestyle appealing.

Chapter 3. Digital Nomads: Outcasts of the Global Bazaar Economy

Tsugio Makimoto and David Manners' (1997) future-oriented manifesto *Digital Nomad* conceptualized the subculture that would come about nearly 20 years later to take on their label as their own identity. While Makimoto and Manners' were writing at the dawn of "telecommuting," they were able to foresee many of the social problems and limitations inherent in this lifestyle. They understood both that such a lifestyle would require a certain level of privilege and financial resources, while also letting companies off the hook in providing full-time employment and benefits for workers. They envisioned tourist hot spots and overcrowding, as well as how white-collar professionals could be freed while service workers were more location-based than ever. They understood that computer technical workers would have the best opportunity for remote work, as well as a high-enough income to enjoy a leisurely lifestyle in ideal destination cities. This chapter examines the types of employment that the participants have engaged in during their short trajectories of employment history, from their entry into the workforce and their current attempts at finding sufficient remote work to pay their bills, while rarely having employee benefits. This chapter asks the detailed questions about what kinds of fields digital nomads are actually employed within, how they find their remote work, and whether they are able to afford their lifestyle over time. The participants are mainly from wealthy, industrialized nations, have many class privileges, but are underemployed compared to what their socioeconomic status would suggest. Their employment is often precarious, although a few are able to maintain full-time employment or the equivalent through their own micro-businesses. While freedom is touted by both industry and workers in the digital nomad context, this lifestyle marks a shift toward insecure employment, and travel that is not differentiated from traditional tourism.

Chapter 4. Bright Sided: Positive Psychology and Its Adaptation to Digital Nomadism

In Chapter 4, digital nomads' use of positive psychology (PP) is examined and the history of the academic subfield is outlined. The entrepreneurial exuberance one finds in corporate seminars – selling the secrets of get rich quick schemes – contextualizes the ideological orientation one finds in digital nomad spaces – both online and in real life (IRL). Platform workers in the gig economy have normalized the requirement of personal branding and the selling of one's self for nearly each gig that they attempt to gain – either via online platforms such as UpWork or by selling self-published e-books in order to promote one's name in the hope of guest speaking invitations to digital nomad conferences. This exuberance for the freedoms provided by the platform economy has CEOs, Silicon Valley executives, and digital nomad lifestyle promoters, equally excited by the possibilities that remote work hypothetically offers. However, as any empirical study of platform and gig workers demonstrates in their finding, this "bright sided" ideology has a very dark other half – as Barbara Ehrenreich (2009) overviews in her ethnographic foray through this transfixing urban jungle of the self-help and motivational speaker subculture. In *Fantasyland: How America Went Haywire*, Kurt Andersen (2017) unearthing a fantastical and mythical belief system, merged with a bootstrap, and protestant work ethic mixture, that makes Americans particularly susceptible to those in the business of selling dreams and fantasy. The lifestyle portrayed is in contrast to the realities of American workers' shrinking real wages and benefits. These authors provide a historical and cultural framework from which to understand the striking appeal of the digital nomad lifestyle to otherwise economically struggling millennials. This chapter overviews the ideological orientation of digital nomad lifestyle marketers in contrast to the empirical findings of actual employment and income as reported by the participants, which does not reinforce the possibility of easily earning "passive money" while one sleeps in Chiang Mai, Thailand.

Chapter 5. Laptops, Sunscreen, Surfboards, and Selfies: Travel, Tourism, and Leisure Practices of the Digital Nomads

This chapter overviews key concepts about the digital nomad lifestyle as it pertains to leisure, the practices in which the participants engage, their ideological understanding of leisure, and the overlap between their prioritized leisure-lifestyle, versus that of their employment, often pushed to the background of their constructed narratives. Selling their life of leisure on social media platforms becomes another way in which they continuously market themselves, always hungry for clients. Indeed, a large part of their leisure is also spent online, constructing their idealized Instagram image while consuming that of others. This chapter overviews the digital nomad lifestyle around the themes of privilege, inequality, and leisure. Robert Stebbins' (2018) concept of serious leisure provides one theoretical perspective, in addition to other sociological theories of leisure, work, and community.

Chapter 6. Seeking Same: Digital Nomads Seek Community

Once digital nomads leave their home countries on their global travel, they often become isolated, lonely, and seek out a community. This chapter explores how digital nomads maintain social connections online, in temporary convergences with the larger digital nomad community, and their relationships to the locals in the locations in which they travel and live. For those who are able to create a location-independent career via the portal of their laptop, leisure activities, including romance, can orient decisions around geographic travel and location. This chapter looks at how digital nomads organize their relationships – romantic, entrepreneurial, friendships, and in community with other nomadic travelers – within their mobile lifestyle. This examination will contextualize the social lives of digital nomads within the sociology literature of family, online dating, community, and leisure.

Chapter 7. Marginalized Identities, Social Justice, and Volun-tourism

The tourism industry overwhelmingly markets to a middle-class white demographic, and this includes the subculture of digital nomadism. Searching Instagram for #digitalnomad will lead one to images of many bikini-clad young, beautiful white women on the beach, with an inspirational quote under her smiling image. About 20% of the images will be of muscular white men presented as engaged in some physical activity, or drinking beer, also with an inspirational quote under his image. However, one must add additional qualifying terms to find images of travelers of color, solo women, LGBT folks, and images of travelers with disabilities. This chapter overviews these marginalized communities within the travel community and how they may have different issues and draws for travel and tourism as their normative white counterparts. Participants speak to the issue of traveling and identity and how their experiences may differ from the white male market.

Chapter 8. Digital Nomads as Canaries in the Coalmine: Disruption and the Future of Work and Leisure

In this chapter, the future of digital nomadism is contextualized in the larger socioeconomic perspective, written at the peak of the 2020 pandemic, which devastated global economies, unemployed millions of workers, and slashed government budgets. Yet, these fallouts represent decades of slashing of social spending, not an inevitable outcome, as small and progressive nations took a different path out of the pandemic. As more office workers moved to remote work overnight, or were laid off, the competition for remote work skyrocketed at the same time that it became a possibility on a large-scale. On the other hand, once travel bans are lifted post-pandemic, more people may move out of dense, urban environments and even move to other countries. The lifestyle may become even more popular in response to the pandemic and other environmental disasters. Tourism is critiqued as an industry that has significant environmental and social impact in the destination locations, which are not immune from protests by local residents against the influx of mass tourism.

Chapter 1

Digital Nomads, Liquid Modernity, and the COVID-19 Pandemic

Introduction

Zygmunt Bauman's (2007) "liquid modernity" – his term to capture the perspective that society was becoming less totalizing and more prone to swift changes or non-linear progressions. Bauman emphasizes an important shift in this society, marking an epoch change, the movement of people from being producers, to consumers. The shift from the gold standard took the material backing out of currency – it shifts to an empty signifier unattached to a material reality. And companies have a powerful role as "persons" in United States law, with the corporate charter to focus solely on maximizing profits, and the larger political will is friendly to bending regulatory laws in their favor (Winkler, 2014). How are workers to position themselves in an economic context where corporations hold all of the power over employee rights, in the American case? The melting of the Keynesian ideal of full and lifelong employment gives way to the gig economy, in which jobs are unpaired from full-time security, benefits, and a future. Each day is its own financial hustle for the micro-entrepreneur. Bauman states that the nomad is the perfect citizen of the liquid society, a stranger in their own land, wandering to find a place for themselves. However, this nomad follows in previously established pathways of tourism often following histories of colonialism, especially in the developing nations. Digital nomads are not refugees, but Westerners with strong passports and resources, just not enough to live as comfortably in their own land as in someone else's. And the COVID-19 pandemic represents one potential crisis of the liquid times, Naomi Klein's concept of "disaster capitalism," is apparent in this pandemic outcome, the outcomes of which always benefit the richest. This chapter overviews Bauman's (2007) liquid society as a theoretical concept that can help make sense of neoliberalism, the gig economy, and worker's rights.

Digital Nomads Living on the Margins:
Remote-Working Laptop Entrepreneurs in the Gig Economy, 13–21

Published under exclusive licence by Emerald Publishing Limited
doi:10.1108/978-1-80071-545-520211002

Liquid Society

Zygmunt Bauman's (2007) concept of liquid modernity, as opposed to the concept of post-modernity, is defining a new and distinct epoch. Institutions and concepts of modernity forge onward, hollowed, their promises no longer bearing fruit, but such facts go overlooked as the gaze is directed not toward the factual, but toward the illusion. The workplace and the school retain the organizational similarity to the mass factory, even though industrial production has left the United States decades before. Our expectations still reside in a Keynesian era, even as the austerity of neoliberalism erases such social protections, we remain fixated on the promises of functional government and workers' rights. Time is liquid precisely because it does not hold its shape. Social forms are liquid "because they decompose and melt faster than the time it takes to cast them, and once they are cast for them to set" (Bauman, 2007, p. 1). We see global despots quickly consolidate their power and control, ensuring their continued domination, at the expense of slashing the survival of millions. Bauman (2012) warns us: "Abandon all hope of totality, future as well as past, you who enter the world of fluid modernity" (p. 21). Not only can people not secure their future paths and that of their children, but even government and corporations cannot plan beyond their next quarter-statement report. As current governments and businesses attempt to plan for multiple different future outcomes of how to maintain profits during times of pandemic and climate catastrophe – we will remain in this liquid uncertainty. Society is abandoned by the state and left to the "inherently unpredictable market forces and/or are left to the private initiative and care of individuals" (Bauman, 2007, p. 2). One major transition that has taken place in late modernity is that "society engages its members primarily in their capacity as consumers rather than producers" (Bauman, 2012, p. 76). Whereas those of previous generations defined themselves based on their professional or employment status. Now, individuals must assess themselves from the perspective of a variety of identity-options, a shopping market of potential identifications, but always from an uncertain, shifting terrain. Bauman offers,

> Being modern means being perpetually ahead of oneself, in a state of constant transgression … it also means having an identity which can exist only as an unfulfilled project. In these respects, there is not much to distinguish between the plight of our grandfathers and our own. (2012, p. 28)

The nomad becomes the iconic character of liquid times – a tourist in their own country, a wandering question mark on the global stage of signification.

One of the strongest holdovers from modernity is the logic and relentless drive of industrial capitalism, coupled with the shriveling defenses of the state against such ravages on the workforce and environment. Neoliberal logic sets its sights upon taking public goods and turning them into private profit (Aronowitz & DiFazio, 2010).

In 1971, Richard Nixon's decision to "unpeg the dollar from precious metals entirely, eliminate the international gold standard, and introduce the system of floating currency regimes has dominated the world economy ever since" (Graeber, 2012, p. 53). Decoupling currency from tangible backing and regulations eventually would give rise to speculative finance and increasingly extreme market volatility (Feher, 2018; Geiselberger, 2017). This development dovetails with privatization of public goods and the increasing indebtedness of individuals (Graeber, 2012; Lazzarato, 2011). Indebtedness as social practice tethers citizens to a corporate controlled life. But, Lazzarato (2011) argues, it is not the free market giving rise to finance, it is that of "injections of astronomical sums of public money" to keep capitalism alive. Through multiple cycles of bailouts that continuously shift wealth from the public to the billionaire class, workers also lose more than money, they lose safety protections (Davis, 2009).

Liquid Employment

The height of affluence for middle-class Americans peaked in the early 1970s and has been in decline ever since. Wages have flat-lined while corporate profits have exploded (Reich, 2013). The technological revolution has contributed to the vast downsizing of the workforce. Once manufacturing provided stable employment for the working class, it was then offshored to other countries for cheaper labor costs and fewer environmental restrictions. The technological revolution allows for some remote work, which could potentially expand corporate access to the global workforce. Touted by proponents as "freedom" for workers to "be their own boss," the reality reveals a marked lowering of worker income. The gig economy simply does not pay well enough. Makimoto and Manners (1997) did predict that technological skills would be important to achieve "location independence," in addition to the need for a "healthy bank account." Indeed, technology contributes to freedom, but the reality shows the opposite. Technology has increased surveillance of all kinds, including those of workers and their data, in addition to fierce propaganda campaigns transported via social media. As Wood (2005) argues, of all the trajectories of technology and society intersections, with the potential for liberation, is instead, "simply a new and rapidly growing 'phase of capitalist accumulation and commodification' " (p. 56).

The Gig Economy

"Late capitalist society is engaged in a long-term historical process of destroying job security, while the virtues of work are ironically and ever more insistently being glorified" (Aronowitz et al., 1998, p. 40). As workers receive fewer wages and benefits, their productivity continuously rises, and the powers of surveillance over their activity are also continuously expanding. The worker is increasingly tethered to their computer regardless of whether they work for a single employer or an app. Rather than relying on a boss' recommendation letter, platform workers accrue client ratings and recommendations, which have a strong impact on their future access to the platform. As Gandini (2016a, 2016b) and E. B. Duffy (2017) find in their empirical research on freelance remote workers and aspirational workers, their online reputation means everything for their career trajectory. Negative reviews can have an impact on one's ability to access future work, thus workers must stress over their interactions with each client (De Stefano, 2016, p. 18).

Application-based employers such as Uber and TaskRabbit, are "almost entirely a small number of technology firms backed by large amounts of venture capital" (Slee, 2017, p. 16). Needless to say, such corporate models aim to achieve high profits, not worker freedom. Arun Sundararajan (2016) is a proponent of what he terms "the sharing economy," and based on his interviews with top corporate leaders, he admits that such an economy will alter employment as we know it:

> Crowd based capitalism could radically transform what it means to have a job. Our regulatory landscape will be reshaped. Our social safety net, often funded by corporate employment, will be challenged. The way we finance, produce, distribute, and consume goods, services, and urban infrastructures will evolve. (loc. 244)

He continues:

> Important worker protections like health coverage, insurance against workplace injuries, paid vacations, a stable income, and other safeguards often provided or guaranteed by large institutional employers will need to come from other sources. (loc. 4196)

Corporations and governments work together – or fail to regulate – such exploitation of workers. While corporations race to create new and questionable practices of business models and employment, the state is slow to keep pace with regulations. Thus, businesses operate without regulation for years before their models are challenged in the courts. A. Sundararajan (2016) admits that freelancers cannot live off of their meager salaries but brushes off the responsibility – or coupling of work with payment – suggestion that "other sources," that is, the government, will have to make up for the lack created by the companies. However, neoliberal policies have decimated government budgets with underfunding, coupled with crises of pandemics and environmental disasters. Makimoto and Manners (1997) foresaw this outcome,

> Project working makes for high temporary rates of pay followed by financial insecurity, in contrast to remaining for a lifetime at one company in secure employment with predictable pay patterns. (loc. 1701)

The mechanization of app work also has an impact on workers' experience. De Stefano (2016) points out it "can 'distort' the perception businesses and customers may have of these workers and significantly contribute to a perceived dehumanization of their activity" (p. 8). Just as some employment sectors, such as translation, are being replaced by technology, human workers are compared against these automated performances. This translates into work intensification (Kelliher & Anderson, 2010).

Let us return to A. Sundararajan's (2016) idealistic spin on the outcomes of "the sharing economy":

> A growing number of people worry if this is an early glimpse into a future of work with less reliable benefits and more uncertainty about where your next paycheck is coming from. Of course, it is not immediately clear that this future is inferior. Perhaps the flexibility and fluidity of contracting through digital platforms rather than working a day job can be empowering. (p. 329)

Rosenblat (2018) points out in his critique of "Uberland" that such upstarts "rely on three poetic fables: the myth of the economic value of 'sharing,' the myth of technological exceptionalism, and the myth of glamorized millennial labor" (p. 30). Newspaper and magazine articles touting the "freedom" and potential glamor of freelance work are perceiving it through rose-colored glasses of privilege. The illusion created by Sundararajan requires an unspoken Universal Basic Income (UBI) – that is, "benefits would have to come from elsewhere." It requires a wage large enough to provide Tim Ferriss's (2009) promised "4-Hour Workweek." "It's ultimately political" writes Graeber (2018, p. 266) on why the labor landscape is arranged as it is. Traditional pressures for government regulations have been slow to develop but are important contributions to hinder the ravaging impacts of the platform economy.

Schor and Attwood-Charles (2017) have conducted empirical research on platform workers and have witnessed the extent of how such employment options have contributed to increased inequality and lower incomes for workers. They state:

> By making cheap labor available at the click of a finger, these platforms and apps are leading to a world in which lower income people are deployed to perform everyday tasks for the more fortunate, whether it is delivering a latte in a rainstorm or picking up groceries. (Schor & Attwood-Charles, 2017, p. 9)

This makes workers vulnerable on many levels: "physical risk, legal risk, and platform risk" (Schor & Attwood-Charles, 2017, p. 9). Platform workers may find themselves acting as drivers in a drug run, managing drunk or unruly clients in their cars, receive damages to their property, and so on, without the company adequately addressing their role in the encounter. The platform economy sells its business as one of technology and providing connections with sellers and clients, but the companies remove themselves from responsibility of what these encounters may bring. Such a system is creating an environment in which marginalized workers contribute all of their time and energy into making meager wages, while providing all of their own resources, and risk (Schor, 2017). Livingston (2016) points out that "almost half of employed adults in this country are eligible for food stamps" (p. 2). Both sides of the platform economy – from the proponents such as Sundararajan to critics such as Schor, agree that the vast majority of platform workers are not making a living wage. And both sides even state the need for a UBI. This shifts responsibility from corporations to properly compensate their workers, to the social programs of the government – another instance of corporate welfare. Yet, the government itself is shrinking from lack of corporate taxes paid. Aronowitz and DiFazio (2010) points to the importance of having "a political and social commitment to a national guaranteed income that is equal to the historical level of material culture" (p. 353). But this is not the direction that our political climate is headed. Instead, a strengthening of the labor movement and social justice movements are imperative to fight this ever-increasing power of the corporations. And while the state is often not the specific target for some of these employment changes, collective action can be targeted instead at the platform itself and its reach.

Neoliberal Leisure and Neocolonial Tourism

Digital nomadism inverts the work-leisure hierarchy and places leisure objectives ahead of employment location. Leisure and consumerism reflect the new economy based on consumption-over-production. Previously identified through one's place in the workforce, now individuals can define themselves more directly through their consumption practices. For digital nomads, this is their travel exploits, as represented on their social media posts. The pathways of contemporary travel follow along historical pathways of colonial encounters. While digital nomads use the word "nomad," they are not nomadic in the definitional sense of a member of a people who move seasonally to herd animals. Nor are they – like the vast majority of contemporary nomadic people – refugees, fleeing war, famine, oppressive governmental action, or persecution. Also distinctive from the global population, digital nomads have powerful passports that allow them to travel to nearly every country on the globe. The remanence of colonialism continues to contribute to current instability and displacement (Green, 2020a; Kaplan, 1996). Tourism and travel follow the pathways of expanding Western capitalism (Kaplan, 1996, p. 3). While under colonialism, Western nations extracted resources from other nations. Under contemporary tourism, Western multinational corporations establish and profit from hotels and tourism infrastructure that does not trickle down to benefit the local population, outside of service employment (Cole, 2016; F. F. Taylor, 1993). Indeed, while tourists may enjoy the finest services in town, including clean water and garbage disposal, the local population may not be as fortunate (Cole, 2016, p. 43; Gmelch, 2012, p. 23). Developing a tourism economy and other export-oriented activities are often promoted for development by the international lenders and other power holders, at the expense of local people who go without (Munshi, 2006). In the Caribbean, as its plantation economy lessened, it then was promoted as a tourist spot for Americans and other Westerners (Pattullo, 2005). But the Caribbean does not control its own tourism economy, especially the cruise ship industry, airline routes, and hotel chains (Alexander, 2005; Munshi, 2006; Urry & Larsen, 2011). Furthermore, tourism drives up the price of land, food, and imports, making it more difficult for locals to afford than traveling Westerners (Gmelch, 2012). Hospitality industries have to also sell tourists on the welcoming nature of the local population, even if that means it needs to be extracted with some force by the government or industries. For example, Alexander (2005) writes about how in the Bahamas, the tourism ministry "initiated a major smile campaign in which Bahamians were urged to remind themselves to be courteous to tourists by wearing smile buttons. But Bahamians refused to smile" (p. 55). This can have a further, more sinister connotation of hospitality and service from locals as sexual availability is implied to attract tourism, which has a distinctly gendered outcome (Munshi, 2006). Tourism objectifies locals, reducing them to a service provider and commodity for Western travelers who come to inhabit a sense of entitlement in such places and over such people.

Liquid Modernity and the COVID-19 Pandemic

In their application of a liquid-modern perspective to the COVID-19 pandemic, Doyle and Conboy (2020) argue that a global pandemic disruption is the perfect example of liquid modernity. Doyle and Conboy (2020) state:

> Liquid modernity prioritizes mobility over rootedness, flexibility over rigidity, adaptability over endurance, ephemerality over durability and responsiveness over restraint. Innovation creates the liquid space for further innovation, while concomitantly downgrading or rejecting the original theory, structure, objective, technology or person. However, we remain solidly predisposed to the imposition of order and control upon conditions that are now necessarily liquid and mutable. (p. 2)

Bauman (2000) argues that power is separated from political agency and resides largely in technological networks, where it can be utilized outside of public understanding of the processes. Thus, the pandemic provides an opportunity for what Naomi Klein (2007) calls "disaster capitalism." In this particular instance of the COVID-19 pandemic, Klein comments in an interview that for the United States in particular, it is the combination of the worst-case scenario of President Trump's mismanagement of the disaster, the lack of a public healthcare system, and lack of worker protections that combines in a trifecta of devastation for a large percentage of Americans (Solis, 2020). Such disasters provide an opportunity for those in power to exploit the situation quickly for their own benefit. In the United States, the $2.2 trillion-dollar Coronavirus Aid, Relief, and Economic Security Act (CARES Act) passed in late March 2020, put guardrails in place to ensure oversights on limits on stock buybacks and caps on executive compensation – however, it was not enforced (Abramson, 2020). Billionaires benefited greatly from the pandemic, most especially the online giants of platform economies and online sales, such as Amazon, Netflix, Google, Apple, and Zoom achieved incredible wealth gains (Kelly, 2020). Meanwhile, those deemed "essential workers" were placed in danger as they worked in health care, selling groceries, delivering products, and working in restaurants. This overwhelmingly impacted the working class, poor, and people of color. Technological innovations had adapted people to swift changes and those companies with the most to gain quickly moved to capture the new markets of online commerce. Those countries that took a hands off approach to the pandemic, such as Sweden, the United States, and Brazil, represent an example of the "liquid" approach of controlling the pandemic, with China representing the "solid" approach of centralized control (Qi, Karlsson, Sallmen, & Wyss, 2020). Reminiscent of Haraway's (1991) "cyborg," infusing technology and humanity, we now have the Alibaba-developed, and Chinese government supported "Alipay Health Code" phone application, which can track citizens and their interactions with potential COVID-19 positive cases, and such applications can apply to extreme surveillance, especially once embedded and adapted. Doyle and Conboy (2020) warn us that the liquidity of citizens providing voluntary data within the European Union, assuming an ideal citizen engaged in their civil responsibilities, is contrasted with the "rampant, privatized individualism that erodes genuine mutual interest" (p. 5).

Conclusion

In this chapter, Zygmunt Bauman's (2007) concept of liquid modernity is introduced as a theoretical framework to understand both the socioeconomic context of the platform economy and the current COVID-19 pandemic disruption that provides a good example of this concept. In this view of society, institutions of modernity are hallowed, and their Keynesian promises long stunted. The austerities of neoliberalism create an economy of workers' rights decimated, while governments and corporations provide a revolving door for the same players to write policy and apply such gains to their own corporate self-interest. The nomad becomes the iconic character of liquid times – a wandering question mark of globalization. In the United States, the early 1970s may be considered the peak for workers' rights, since which such benefits have been in a long decline. The gig economy has taken hold in the context of few rights for workers and platforms that write their own rules, obscure their functions from the public, and impose these life-changing adaptions upon society, and when challenged in courts, they fight viciously for their right to exist and their right to classify workers as freelancers. Such cases have been filed around the world with varying effects. A great deal of the literature on the gig economy focuses on the benefits as touted by those at the top, the platform designers and benefactors. Only a few studies focus on the impacts of workers (E. B. Duffy, 2017; Gandini, 2016a; Schor, 2017; Schor & Attwood-Charles, 2017). Within such a context, those Westerners with strong passports and slim full-time employment options still have opportunities such as digital nomadism, where they can work online and live in an affordable country. Contemporary tourism follows the pathways of previously colonized countries, especially in Southeast Asia, where digital nomads like to gather in large numbers. While they deny they are merely vulgar tourists, digital nomad behavior does little to reinforce such distinctions, as they live among other Westerners, in Western-style accommodations, and pay little attention to the local people, culture, or language. Thus, they also contribute to displacement of locals who face higher prices with the influx of an infrastructure aimed at tourism. The COVID-19 pandemic provides an example of liquid modernity in that "all that is solid melts into air." The pandemic allowed for sudden changes that were previously unimaginable – remote school, remote work, bailout funds re-routed to corporations (Doyle & Conboy, 2020). Bauman's (2007) liquid society provides us with a theoretical framework for understanding this socioeconomic shift in our global society.

Chapter 2

Western Millennials: Demographics and Socioeconomic Status

Introduction

Taking the liquid society context, this chapter examines the particular population demographics that will find themselves working in this fluctuating environment and what kind of future they can expect. First, overviewing the overall context of the millennial generation, the participants' background stories illuminate their family's socioeconomic status and their own anticipated trajectory. Millennials as a whole have increased opportunities for higher education and optimism toward the future, which often does not provide the anticipated employment opportunities. However, the digital nomad millennials leverage one of their privileges – a strong passport and currency. Western digital nomad communities and gatherings are often predominantly racially white. This points toward the leveraging of another privileged characteristic. The participants also came from families of some means, at least enough to assist with the buying of an airplane ticket or providing a loan in an emergency. The vast majority were college educated. This chapter also oversamples women's and LGBT voices, in order to highlight stories often overshadowed by studies focused on white and male digital nomads. This chapter does attempt to bring perspective to a wider demographic of digital nomads in order to understand their unique challenges in employment and leisure. The background of the participants will be explored: family wealth, social class, nationality, education, debt/asset, gender and sexual orientation, political engagement and workforce participation. Finally, this chapter contextualizes how the neoliberal national context and shrinking social safety net makes this lifestyle appealing. Thus, shortcomings of the home country and rising costs of living squeeze millennials to the point where they consider individualist options for surviving and thriving. While the individual situations vary, the lifestyle must be understood in the contemporary neoliberal politics and economic expectations of younger generations.

Digital Nomads Living on the Margins:
Remote-Working Laptop Entrepreneurs in the Gig Economy, 23–32

doi:10.1108/978-1-80071-545-520211003

The Demographics and Social Context of the Western, Millennial Generation Participants

Marketing websites present the digital nomad subculture as one that is open to "anyone." However, there are demographic markers that the majority of these lifestyle participants have in common. Other demographic markers make it nearly impossible to join this subculture.

The interviewees are primarily millennials or younger, with only four in their 40s. Twenty-two of the participants are in their 30s. Twelve participants are in their 20s. This demonstrates that in order to be a digital nomad, one should be post-college, have some minimal work experience, and yet be unencumbered with responsibilities such as childrearing. Only one participant was a current college student.

All of the participants possess a strong passport. Three participants hold passports from Central America and Nigeria – but all three of these participants also held a European passport (Spain and Ireland). Thus, none of the participants held a passport from only a developing nation. Specifically, the participants were of the following nationalities: 17 Americans (two with additional Ireland and Brazil passports); six were UK passport holders (two additionally held in United States and Germany passports); 1 Austrian, 2 Australians, 6 Canadians, and 2 Central Americans (paired with Spanish passports). Notably, there were no participants from Latin America (who did not hold EU passports); nor from Africa or Asia. Therefore, nationality was a crucial aspect of becoming a digital nomad.

Language is also crucial for digital nomadism. Most of the community gatherings are in English; with a large subset of German speakers. Twenty-two of the interviewees spoke English only. Nine participants spoke English, in addition to one other language (one Dutch, one Portuguese, three German, one Spanish, and one Hindi). Two individuals spoke two languages, five participants spoke three languages, and two spoke four languages. Very few participants spoke a language that was not directly tied to their cultural heritage. Only two Spanish learners were expanding their linguistic abilities beyond their background. As people who consider themselves global citizens and long-term travelers, their reliance on English speaking, and their resistance to learning a language, was significant, and demonstrated their reliance on personal privilege and historically colonial languages to navigate their global travel.

Racial Identity

Twenty-five of the participants are white, five are black, two are white Hispanic, one is Arab American, two are Asian, and three are mixed-race (Pakistan/Euro, British white/Japanese, and white/Filipino). Digital nomads are usually from white-dominated societies and travel and stay with other nomads of similar racial, ethnic, and national backgrounds, such as in co-living and coworking spaces. Amada Lewis (2004) examines how it is that groups become all-white, even when race is rarely spoken of:

> Although numerous all-white groups are not explicitly racial, their racial composition is not an accident but is a result of whites'

> status as members of a passive social collective whose lives are shaped at least in part by the racialized social system in which they live and operate. (p. 627)

Lewis continues, "the silence that so often surrounds whiteness leaves white racial selves unexamined and leaves them unchallenged as norms" (p. 642). This reproduction of white racial norms is especially disappointing in a global traveler context in which members supposedly aspire to learn of other cultures and places. However, nomads often seek out fellow travelers in which to engage, rather than integrating into their current locations. This allows nomads to further ignore the workings of race. For travelers of color, they cannot avoid global racism (Lucal, 1996). As Eichstedt (2001) demonstrates in her data, whites rely on their "interactions with people of color" to learn about racial dynamics and white privilege (p. 455). Griffin (1998) found that when students were asked:

> to contemplate their own whiteness, we are likely to get one of three initial responses: angry resistance, which seems to betoken that to be called white is to be attacked; avoidance and digression into abstraction; or blankness (a distinguishing feature of whiteness), which struggles to grasp the concept, to see what has been rendered invisible. (p. 4)

One of the things that has been rendered invisible by this unspoken white norm is the experience of non-white nomads who have to navigate racism while traveling. Hegemonic whiteness informs most of leisure studies and the engagement of leisure and travel (Spracklen, 2013). For

> non-white, non-western, non-elite people who do try to travel to the west face problems with visas and crossing borders, and are labelled as dangerous, unwanted economic migrants and potential asylum-seekers. (Spracklen, 2013, p. 174)

And when people of color who are citizens of Western nations travel internationally, they might be assumed to come from a non-Western country, or seen as service workers, but not as British residents on holiday (Urry & Larsen, 2011). Because of this white racial hegemony in the travel industry, travelers of color must seek out additional information sources to examine racism in their target destinations. Such considerations are often overlooked by white travelers or event organizers.

Parents' Wealth and Socioeconomic Background

The participants are primarily from middle- and upper-middle-class homes. The majority of the participants' parents have earned bachelor's degrees. Their parents had clear gender normative divisions of labor, both in the household and in the workplace. Fourteen of the participants' fathers worked in the fields of business, finance, engineering, or computer programming. Three participants' fathers were medical doctors. Six were blue-collar workers. Four were in the military. Of the mother/wives, eight were housewives who quit their pink-collar jobs in order to attend to childcare, and some had worked in banking, as teachers, or in retail. Three were nurses. Four were mid-level office workers. Two were engineers. Beyond their employment positions, such families had other resources from which their children materially benefited, and which contributed to their ability to be a digital nomad.

As millennials are the least resourced generation of the last century, family assistance is a boon, further exasperating the class and racial divisions among millennials, from those with less wealth transfer (Hagerman, 2018). Worth (2018) defines wealth transfer as:

> [...] money – given to Millennials for education, a down payment for a house, or to support day-to-day life. One of the most common (and expected) forms of support that Millennials identify is money to partly or fully support college, undergraduate or graduate education. (p. 112)

As millennials leave the parental household for college (or do not), we see the division between social classes emerge. Some do not attend college. Others attend college with full parental tuition support. And yet others do not have parental support and thus incur student debt or work full time while attending college. Some are able to live at home with their parents and save on rent money, while others must support their own expenses (Worth, 2018). In the European Union, young people are also leaving the parental home much later than previous decades in all of the member states (Eurostat, 2015, p. 10). When millennials do live outside of the parental home, they are living with other peers and are much less likely to marry (Mawhorter, 2018, p. 202). For millennials in Thailand in comparison, 63% still live with parents, and do so until they marry, traditionally. However, there is a growing trend of young adults renting apartments in urban centers such as Bangkok, while working in the CBD (The Nation Thailand, 2017). This shows the imbalance of family resources that can contribute to a young person's ability to be a digital nomad.

Social Class and Privilege

In Makimoto and Manners (1997) *Digital Nomad* manifesto, they foresaw that the lifestyle required funding:

> the main facilitator for the Digital Nomad is a credit card backed by a healthy bank balance. Nomadism will not, for a while yet be an inexpensive lifestyle. As well as reducing materialism, the rise of nomadism could dilute the power of nationalism. (loc. 1737)

The digital nomad lifestyle seeks to maximize the privilege allocation of younger citizens – by transporting them to a country in which their status becomes elevated in comparison. Privilege offers a

> false protection so that they never see themselves, the devastation they wreck or their accountability to it. Privilege and superiority blunt the loss that issues from enforced alienation and segregations of different kinds. (Alexander, 2005, p. 2)

Scott (2012) reinforces this narrative by pointing out that:

> Those of us who "won" this race are the lifetime beneficiaries of opportunities and privileges that would not likely otherwise have come our way. We are also are likely to carry a lifetime sense of entitlement, superiority, accomplishment, and self-esteem that comes from this victory. (p. 72)

While white Western millennials have been raised with this sense of privilege and entitlement, especially in relation to the global population, this can reinforce systemic power inequalities inherent in the pathways of postcolonial leisure, travel, and gentrification (Hagerman, 2018). While such Western youth may not feel privileged in their home countries, their relative advantage in Thailand is immense. Back home in the United States, millennials have the least wealth – 3%. When baby boomers were the equivalent age, they held 21% of the national wealth (Hoffower, 2019). Currently, Generation X holds 16% of US wealth (Hoffower, 2019). Millennial households are the largest generation-cohort accounted for in American poverty rates: 5.3 million in 2016, compared to 5.0 million baby boomers and 4.2 million Generation X households (Fry, 2017).

In contrast, for millennials in developing nations – they are even worse off. Thailand's household income per capita reached $3,322 USD in 2017 ("Thailand Household Income per Capita," 2017). In Argentina, poverty nationwide rose to 35.4% in 2019, leaving a large number of households unable to properly feed themselves and provide basic necessities (Poverty rose to 35.4% in first half of 2019, 2019). This further demonstrates the difficulties that millennials from developing nations would have to overcome to achieve a nomadic lifestyle.

Debts, Assets, and Income

The participants of this study were not overly burdened with student debt compared to their larger generational cohort, which holds the largest percentage of student loan debt. Nineteen of the participants had no student debt. Eighteen did have student debt. Four were in deferment. Only four participants had significantly high student debt, with the highest being $130,000. For the Australians and British citizens, their student loan debt was a small tax taken from their paycheck – and if they lacked a paycheck – they were not penalized or charged. The Americans had the highest rates of student loan debt, highest payments, and were unable to stop payment if unemployed (outside of deferment). In the United States, it is not possible to have student loans forgiven, even in a bankruptcy, and one's social security or disability payments can be garnished for repayment demands. Baudrillard (2005) comments on this debt to society:

> The illusionism is truly remarkable: society appears to extend credit to you in exchange for a formal freedom, but in reality, it is you who are giving credit to society, alienating your future in the process. (p. 174)

In the United States, millennials with a bachelor's degree or higher are best positioned to make median annual earnings of $56,000 in 2018; but for those with "some college," they reported making $36,000, lower than the baby boomers graduates who were making $38,900 in 1982 (Bialik & Fry, 2019). In 2012, the youngest three age cohorts had an average debt-to-asset ratio above 100% (Walks, Simone, & Hawes, 2018, p. 76).

Millennials have different levels of debts globally. Germany continues to provide very affordable or free higher education to its population (Bruckmeier & Wigger, 2014). In China, tuition averages around $2,000 USD annually and thus does not contribute to student loan debt. The government subsidy for education is estimated around $250 billion annually (Lim, 2016). In Australia, young people are buying homes at a vastly lower rate than previous generations (Rayner, 2016). And in the UK, new generations of workers are not being offered the defined benefit pension schemes that their parents received (Brown et al., 2017).

Gender and Sexuality

The majority of participants of this study were women: 33 of 38. This sampling orientation attempts to focus the data collection on issues of gender and employment by examining specifically which kinds of work women engage in comparison to men. Within the popular literature, there is a stereotype of digital nomads as "bromads," – white, testosterone-fueled, millennial males who party, dominate space, offend women, and engage in male-dominated leisure interests, such as sports. Creating such a stereotypical image of the community can work to replicate such embodiments while at the same time repelling other demographic groups. Previous studies have centered men in the digital nomad subculture, so this study attempts to bring some attention to gender outcomes in the community. For sexual orientation demographics, 30 of the participants identified as straight. Five identified as gay or lesbian, and three identified as bisexual or fluid. Of 38 participants, 32 were single; albeit 10 were in relationships of varying lengths. Only six were married, and of those, two were getting divorced. Within the heterosexual couples, the male partners had more leverage in selecting this lifestyle and choosing the locations to which they would travel (Haworth, 2014, p. 40). This can be tied to men earning more money, and therefore, their job dictating their location or their financial ability to afford a location may lead the couple to select one place over another.

Having children in the lifestyle is a popular topic to feature at conferences, but the reality is less popular. Only one of the participants had children, and they were adults. All the rest of the participants were childfree. Strikingly, the vast majority were unsure if they *ever* wanted children. Only four were certain they wanted children in the future. Seventeen were unsure if they desired children. Fourteen definitely did *not* want children. Desiring fewer children is a growing trend among millennials compared to previous generational cohorts. In 2017, Australia hit its lowest fertility rate of 1.74 ever documented (Australian Institute of Family Studies, 2017; Rayner, 2016). Couples with children across Europe, Canada, the United States, and Russia are becoming a much smaller percentage of the population, under 30%, and in the case of Russia, under 16% (Eurostat, 2015, p. 44). Furthermore, when younger generations have children, it is nearly twice as likely that the birth will be outside of marriage (Eurostat, 2015, p. 10). Disaggregating the data based on racial groups, we see that Asian are the most likely millennials to be married at 48%; whites were second at 48%; Hispanics were at 42%, and blacks were lowest at 24% (Barroso, Parker, & Bennett, 2020).

Educational Attainment

The participants reflect the high educational attainment that is common of millennials across the world. This generation is marked by being the most highly educated (38% in the United States) and yet have lowered opportunities for advancement in the current neoliberal economy (Fry, 2018, p. 54). The participants are perhaps more highly educated than the general population. Only one participant has only a high school education (and was, ironically, the most highly paid individual, with a six-digit salary from a career). Only one participant was a current college student, and three had "some college." The vast majority – 23 of the interviewees – had earned a bachelor's degree. Six had a Juris Doctor law degree. And two had PhDs in chemistry.

For participants in wealthy nations, educational attainment is high, and for developing nations, educational attainments are significantly higher than in the past (OECD Better Life Index Germany, 2020). Costa Rica provides affordable higher education ($200/semester) through the University of Costa Rica (UCR) (Pacific Trade Winds, 2019). Still, half of millennials in Costa Rica do not enter higher education, and yet they are able to earn over $775 USD a month (T. Williams, 2016). In 2006, Argentina passed a National Education Finance Law that mandated that 6% or more of the country's gross domestic product (GDP) be spent on education (Monroy, 2018), and it has the second highest tertiary education enrollments after Chile. In a final example for educational attainment increases, we can turn to China, where the millennial generation is having an impact on nearly every institution and is a huge driver of consumption. Over 90% have a cell phone, two-thirds of all Chinese passport holders are millennials, and they buy more than half of the luxury goods, including their share of the $1,150 billion spent on global travel in 2017 (Kidwai, 2019). For now, Chinese millennials are earning bachelor's degrees at a rate of 25%, but for a nation of its size, the trajectory is considerable. Additionally, Chinese make up the largest nationality of international students with 369,548 in 2018–2019, followed by India, with 202,014, and Korea trails at 52,250 (Duffin, 2019). These students pay some of the highest tuition rates in the United States, making them an important segment of the higher education consumer market. In Australia, there are more than 2 million Chinese students in 2019, with 1.7 in higher education alone, in a country where with the highest rate of international students at one third of all the national student enrollment (Hinton, 2020).

Political Engagement

Overall globally, voting engagement has been on a downward trend since the 1970s, with significant spikes of activity. Generally, engagement increases with age. In post-Soviet countries, there is a large downward voting trend since the first free election post-cold war (Solijonov, 2016, p. 27). Globally, rates of male and female voting levels are nearly equal but disaggregating for countries demonstrates largest gender differences in voting turnout include the areas of the Middle East, North Africa, and Asia, with Pakistan holding the lowest female voting percentage (Solijonov, 2016, p. 31). Out of the 32 Organization for Economic Co-operation and Development (OECD) countries, the United States ranks 26 for general voter turnout (Desilver, 2018). While the youth vote is consistently low, between 2014 and 2018, the three youngest voting cohorts outvoted baby boomers, and older, by several millions for the first time (Cilluffo & Fry, 2019). Japan recently lowered the voting age to 18, which added an extra 2.4 million young people to the vote in the subsequent election of 2016, with an overall turnout rate of 54.7% (Nakatani, 2017). In the 2014 New Zealand general election, an estimated 85% of the eligible voting population turned out, with Māori populations holding the lowest trust in parliament and subsequently, lower political engagement (Voting and Political Participation, 2018). South Africa had a higher voter turnout than the United States at 65.34%, on par with France (67.93%) and Germany (69.1%) and the UK (68.7%) and far above Nigeria (37.1%) (Head, 2019). South Korea saw peak turnout rates in 2020 at 66.2%, the highest since 1992, which had a 71.9 turnout (Hollingsworth & Kwon, 2020). Canada has slightly higher turnout rates than the United States: the Trudeau win was the result of a peak turnout at 68.5%, the highest since 1993 (Rumley, 2019).

Some other democratic countries have taken a different approach by implementing mandatory voting. Two countries that provide such an example include Costa Rica and Australia. Costa Rica recently expanded their voter registration to include expats, and 3.3 million Costa Ricans were registered in 2018, out of the population of 5 million, as the voting requirement holds no penalty for not voting (Sonneland, 2018). Australia also maintains a mandatory voting requirement which was introduced in response to only 55% of Australians voting in the 1922 general election (Wright & Koslowski, 2019). The 2017 marriage equality bill in Australia added many young people to the registration rolls, bringing it to 16.5 million enrolled voters – 96.8%, the highest since Federation (Wright & Koslowski, 2019).

Workforce Participation

In this neoliberal economy, workers face constant stress over losing their job through downsizing, outsourcing, or having their hours or benefits slashed.

Companies are solely responsible to their shareholders with the only aim of increasing profit, and this is often at the expense of the workforce. Germany stands out as one of the few global countries sustaining low unemployment rates even during the recession of 2008 (OECD Better Life Index Germany, 2018). Australia has high wages for workers, as Rayner (2016) reports IT workers can code up to a $93/hourly rate while those working in cash registers can earn $34 and hospitality workers around $31 (p. 322). In Costa Rica, workers are primarily in the service sector at nearly 70%, with 18.37 in industry and 12.33 in agricultural sectors (Plecher, 2020a). In Thailand in 2019, 30.43% of the workers were in the agricultural sector, 23.49 in industry and 46.09 in the service sector (Plecher, 2020b). We can see the divide between developing and industrialized nations can be seen in workplace sectors of agriculture, industry, service, and then the extent of professional white-collar workers. Of these example countries, Thailand has the highest rates of agricultural workers. In contrast, digital nomads, with their taste for Thailand extended stays, can easily outspend the locals on rent and luxury items.

In the UK, one survey found that millennials with full-time employment planned on leaving their jobs in the next several years because of their dissatisfaction (Ritschel, 2018). In 2014, in the United States, 14.4 million workers were self-employed or roughly 10% of the workforce, while the percentage of employees working from home also continues to rise (L. E. Garrett, Spreitzer, & Bacevice, 2017). Self-employed micro-entrepreneurs encounter "millions of micro-contracts," leading to increased insecurity as each new job requires a new bid (Rayner, 2016; Vinodrai, 2018). In contrast to the few at the top of the remote work employment sector, such as Silicon Valley start-up entrepreneurs, there is a vast sea of struggling workers at the low end of the scale (Gandini, 2016b). Such employment insecurity is especially applicable for working women, as more British women than men find themselves in the health, education, or retail sector and work at part-time rates much more often than men (Eurostat, 2015, p. 156; Government Equalities Office, 2019). Women also contribute a great deal of unpaid and unacknowledged domestic labor which contributes to the larger economy. Youth are especially facing higher unemployment numbers than their older generation cohorts (Eurostat, 2015, p. 11). Finally, besides those who struggle to find more meaningful and higher paid employment; others are downshifting in order to have more time to spend with family or to consume less in general (Hamilton & Mail, 2003, p. viii).

Increased Urbanization

In order to access jobs, resources, and leisure pursuits, people are moving to urban environments at an escalating pace globally. In England, millennials are concentrated in London (Brown et al., 2017, p. 3). Furthermore, UK millennials work in wholesale and retail (13.5%), health and social work (12.4%), and education (9.8%), thus making their skills difficult to transition to remote work (Brown et al., 2017, p. 3). Especially in urban areas, millennials are pushed to live together with roommates as few have full-time jobs that can support the range of their expenses (Brown et al., 2017, p. 25). Because of this difficult lifestyle in many Western countries, we can understand the desire for millennials to move beyond such limitations, where their money and privilege can go further (Cohen, Duncan, & Thulemark, 2013, p. 5). Mobility becomes another layer of privilege that can improve one's marketability.

Conclusion

This chapter overviews the socioeconomic status of the millennial generation globally to understand this generation's power and standing in the world. Second, the digital nomad participants are positioned within this larger understanding of their generational situation, paying attention to the particularities of how the participants are able to take on the digital nomad lifestyle. Overall, millennials are the most educated generation to exist, with the highest tertiary education attainment of any generation. However, especially in the United States and UK, high tuition rates and student debt are paired with this educational attainment. For the participants of this study, half of them had student loan debt, but those with excessive debt are unlikely to take on such a lifestyle. Most of the participants were white and Western, and those originating in a developing country often first navigated to become a citizen of a developed country before taking on this lifestyle – thus all of the participants hold a strong passport, as other studies have reaffirmed (Mancinelli, 2020). They were at an age where college had been completed but childrearing or marriages were not yet entered into, and thus they had the free time to travel and market their micro-businesses. They had mostly engaged in entry-level employment, and only a few participants had previously been employed full time or otherwise had received a good salary. This chapter demonstrates, as Makimoto and Manners (1997) predicted, that the digital nomad lifestyle does indeed require some socioeconomic and nationality privileges. While such nomads may think of themselves as lacking in privilege in comparison to older generations in their home countries, their relative privilege in comparison to the country in which they adopt during their travels is immense, thus providing the sense of luxury and lifestyle benefits that come with being a digital nomad.

Chapter 3

Digital Nomads: Outcasts of the Global Bazaar Economy

Introduction

> Like the peddlers in the global bazaar economy, they are also outcasts, either because they are unable to find a corporate job despite their expensive education, or because they had one and got fed up with it. And they are similarly precarious and eke out a modest living, if they earn anything at all. (Arvidsson, 2019, p. 46)

Few of the remote workers work full time with one employer and thus do not have paid sick days, holiday, retirement, and other securities. When work becomes remote, it is easier to outsource as piecework, thus becoming cheaper still. Arvidsson (2019) warns of this transition brought forth in the digital economy as sectors of office workers can be remotely recruited, potentially from distant lands in which wages are far less, and work for brief periods of time, not requiring further commitment from the employer.

In the previous chapter, millennial employment in key countries was examined in order to understand the larger global context of the economy and employment sector for younger workers just entering their careers. In this chapter, we look specifically at the remote work experience of the participants. How do these young adults encounter their short-term, entry-level work options? From this, how do they decide to juggle traveling with remote work? The participants talk about the variety of work they have found in order to maintain their lifestyle. As the participants are more female than male, the employment patterns reflected the larger gender-skewing of them being oriented toward piecework marketing assignments, rather than having training in computer programming. Their employment patterns incurred less salary and were lower skilled than similar male-age workers. Aydogdu (2016) argues that the digital nomad lifestyle:

Digital Nomads Living on the Margins:
Remote-Working Laptop Entrepreneurs in the Gig Economy, 33–44

doi:10.1108/978-1-80071-545-520211004

> can be criticized from a critical feminist perspective for its perpetuation of a "phallo-centric" and technologically-driven notion of progress. This nomad fully embraces the dominant capitalist logic of speeding up the desire for ever-new products and services. Notwithstanding assertions that permanent connectivity, not gadgetry and hyper-mobility, are what counts, the digital nomad strongly retains a male-biased flavor. Toys for the boys. The nomad also reaffirms Enlightenment ideals of hyper-individuality. It re-boxes old identity notions of total personal freedom and autonomy in a trendy term. Rather than perpetually questioning fixed identity categories, as the nomadologists have it, this technologically-driven utilitarian nomad is happy to maximize his own freedom of movement and to optimize personal choices by exerting control. (p. 8)

For the millennial generation, there continues to be a gender distinction in the educational and occupational pursuits of men and women. There has been much handwringing over the small numbers of women in STEM fields, which leads to high-paid employment. Entering male-dominated spaces is perhaps more comfortable for men, and such spaces overlap with those in the digital nomad community, the "technologically-driven and phallo-centric" culture.

Employment History

For new college graduates, it is difficult to land a job in one's chosen field, and they may find themselves back in the service industry (Brundage, 2017). Once graduated from college, young adults are thrust into a competitive job market without the necessary skills. Networking can lead to other opportunities if one has social capital. Participant Alexandra is an Australian who was entering the field of broadcast media:

> I continued with the piecemeal job situation. I had one job that I'd gotten before I finished university, it was at a place called Media Monitors. And the job was listening to broadcast media – radio and TV news – and monitoring it for mentions of any businesses or government departments things, making notes. And then the company would then alert those people and say, "Hey, did you know that you were on morning news?" Then they would sell that clip of broadcast to them. I did that. And it was weird because it was really well-paid, and casual. I could basically get as many hours as I wanted. But they were always at weird times. So, I might have started work at 5:30 in the morning; or worked until midnight. But that really suited me, because I was doing a lot of creative stuff like theatre. Which I did often at university as well.

This indeed is a "weird" employment opportunity, as Alexandra calls it, as it was flexible, casual, and high paid. It taught her marketing skills suited for targeting clients to sell them products that compliments their vanity. This job also provided her with a sizable tax return check, which later provided financial means when she was working in the UK.

Twenty-seven of the participants had short-term and low-level jobs at the beginning of their work lives. Chelse was unable to find a job for months after graduation:

> I tried to find a job anywhere that would take me. This was 2012 and I couldn't get hired at J.C. Penny's. I couldn't get a waitressing job. The market was rough. I was unemployed for six or seven months until I got my first job. I was a social media manager in Charleston, South Carolina. Thank God. Lucky break.

This luck of finding a full-time opportunity in social media would provide her with skills transferable to remote work. Twenty of the participants said that their work skills were gained on the job, as compared to 17 others who said that college did provide them with job skills. Fifteen participants have always had small jobs, gigs, and temporary employment. Taylor was previously an unpaid summer camp volunteer during her college years. But camp led to an opportunity that inspired her to later become nomadic:

> I simply was volunteering at a camp I had volunteered at for 4 years in a row. It's a camp for people with disabilities. They said, "Oh, one of the counsellors from the '80s – one of the volunteers – started a similar camp in Guatemala. She's looking for volunteers from our camp because you already know how to take care of people with disabilities. It doesn't matter if you know Spanish. If you want to go and pay for the flights, it is a 10-day vacation in Guatemala with people with disabilities." I was like, "Sign me up. Sure." I went by myself and it just completely changed my life. I flew back on the plane. I was like, "I have to quit teaching. I have to do something to get back into Central America again." I was completely changed forever.

Out of the 38 participants, 20 have had, or have "good jobs," or high-skilled, well-paid, full-time employment. This was especially true for the men who had computer programming employment like Nate:

> I graduated from Georgia Tech. I was promoted to full-time at a company for about a year or year-and-a-half and then I moved to Santa Monica, California. I originally stayed remote with them for a little while before I even really understood what remote work was, strangely enough. I only stayed in that job for maybe another 3–6 months. The cost of living in L.A. is a lot more than in Atlanta, Georgia, so I had to find higher-paying employment. It was a little bit of a dark period. I left that job and did some

> freelance work, like software development, and bounced around. I was a little aimless for a while. Then, I got a job at a company that was owned by AOL and got my last full-time job before I became a digital nomad. It was the 6-figure salary, health benefits, 401K, and all the corporate bits to the nines.

For the participants, having a six-figure corporate job for a few years before inevitable layoffs was pretty much peak achievement. From there, someone like Nate could expect to freelance for much less but still make a decent salary.

Only 15 of the participants had previously developed skilled that assisted their transition to a digital nomad lifestyle. Bettina did study media and marketing in school and was able to land jobs that continued to develop her abilities:

> I started in an agency for events and PR. I was working there during my studies. Then, after that, I was a manager of a famous photographer in Austria. I did PR, artist management, event management, social media, and worked a little bit in photography – not taking photos but more like editing, small things. I did that for one-and-a-half years. Then, I moved to Amsterdam. I worked in online marketing and sales for about 2 years. A lot of the skills I have right now, I learned myself.

The participants often expressed that they were "lucky" if they were able to network an opportunity or gain some sort of advantage. Full-time jobs implied one had higher-level skills, but these jobs were not expected to last. Layoffs are routine. They simply provide a buffer until the next cycle.

Inspiration for Becoming a Digital Nomad

With a college degree and some work experience, the participants were well situated to discover digital nomadism, as they thought about their future trajectory and desires. The lifestyle is posted widely across social media, a postcard perfect image of millennial success. The websites promise the lifestyle is easy to attain and many jump in first, before finding employment. They arrive at a coworking space in Chiang Mai, Thailand – a digital nomad "hot spot" with the extensive offering of coworking spaces, cafes, affordable Airbnb apartments, and others of the same subculture (Rentschler & Boyle, 2019). The participants were often at a crossroads: college was complete, yet their employment opportunities were lackluster. Chelse found herself in this position on her 25th birthday:

> I was not always remote and, actually, the position was not supposed to be remote at all. But, on my 25th birthday, I had this epiphany. I had been watching this TV show called, *Chasing Life*, about this girl with cancer. She was twenty-five at the time in the TV show. I was like, "Is this it? Am I going to go to work every single day until I die?" Then, I started researching options. I found

> this thing called digital nomadism. I had never heard of it before. Then, the next week, I sat down with my boss and said, "This is what's going to happen. I'm totally cool if you want to fire me. You're not going to find anyone as good as me." I mean, I said it nicer than that. But it was definitely an ultimatum. Thank goodness that they accepted my wild behavior.

Chelse was able to negotiate with her current full-time employer to allow her to work remotely. That job lasted for a while longer until she transitioned into her own remote marketing company. Sara was a bit older when she had a similar realization as that of Chelse:

> I realized that it was not really what I wanted to do. I was not happy with the work/life balance, with the job itself. I had been doing a lot of interviews but wasn't really succeeding at anything. I was trying to make a career change at that point. I decided to take a month off to do some traveling. I traveled for a little over a month. It was my first solo trip. I came back and realized that I really wanted to pursue the idea of being a digital nomad. It was something that I had heard about when I first graduated university but, at the time, in 2012, I wasn't really sure if I had any skill set that allowed me to work online. I kind of put it on the back burner and thought maybe this is something I won't be able to pursue. When it came down, I decided that I really wanted to figure out a way that I would be able to travel and work.

As they were single women with little previous work experience, it was a struggle to fully support themselves. Previous generations, especially the baby boomers, entered a world of possibilities after earning college degrees – and those without degrees easily found well-paid manufacturing work. Millennials are considered the first generation to achieve less than their parents in a century. Women also now outearn men in college degrees, yet gender-based employment discrimination and inequalities persist. Of the participants, a select handful of women were high earners. More often than not, women were subsidized by male partners. This was the case for Jemma:

> My boyfriend and I – who I met working in the marketing agency – had both read *The 4-hour Work Week*, by Tim Ferriss. I was reading this book and I thought, "This could be my life if I just follow what Tim Ferriss is saying here; maybe I could do this all the time. Lie on the beach and be in a nice warm country. Not be in Scotland where it rains all the time and where it costs 5 dollars for a coffee. I could be in Portugal." So, that kind of gave me the motivation. My partner looked into a lot of ways to travel. He discovered house sitting, which is where you go and look after someone else's pets and their home while they go on holiday. So, we signed up for Trusted House

> Sitters and a few other websites. We worked out that in order to do this, we would need to earn about 500 pounds a month to live at our level of lifestyle. We budgeted, we saved money, and we applied for a lot of house sits. So, we started out house sitting, and we did that for nine months in the south of France. At the time, my copywriting business was growing. I was getting more referrals, more clients, more work. My boyfriend actually got in touch with the owners of Trusted House Sitters and they hired him as their SEO consultant and they're paying him a proper salary of 40 thousand pounds a year and he worked remotely. At this point, we realized that we were spending all this time in the day walking dogs, feeding cats, and doing the gardening. We had enough money and could rent a place and make more money working than doing these little tasks and it would pay for itself. So, in 2013, we decided to rent long-term on Airbnb rather than looking for house sits.

Both Jemma and Marta had boyfriends who were technologically driven and had discovered and pursued the lifestyle with milder interest from their female partners. In all the cases of male–female couples, the males far outearned the females (Aydogdu, 2016). This placed them in a more powerful bargaining position within the relationship. While both Jemma and her partner similarly desired the lifestyle, Marta's partner was willing to choose the lifestyle over their relationship:

> It was not my idea, to be absolutely fair. My fiancé – a real nerd – lives online, basically, in work and life. He started encountering articles about the digital nomad movement. We had conversations, mostly drinking wine, but I was always supportive. I loved traveling for holidays – with my friends, this standard way of traveling – but I never took it seriously until we had some problems in our relationship. I had left my job and stayed at home. That didn't work very well for our interactions because I became dependent on him and that's not a very good structure for a relationship to work. He decided that he was going to travel. I said, "I don't want to." That was his understanding, that we have to split up, break up, and he was going to travel. So, we broke up. It took us 2 or 3 weeks. I decided to travel on my own. So, at some point, with a lot of drama, we decided that we loved each other very much and actually wanted to build a life together. So, we created a one-year plan to prepare ourselves for this financially. We bought tickets a year in advance to Chiang Mai. We chose this place because Chiang Mai was the first on the list as the most popular digital nomad destination in the world. So, we decided to go to a place where we will meet nomads and see how it works.

Marta's entry into the lifestyle dismayed her friends and family, who found it a threat once their plan was enacted. The digital nomad lifestyle does challenge traditional pathways to middle-class adulthood that can position them at odds with their peers. Therefore, Marta and her boyfriend headed to the digital nomad hot spot in search of community. In these coworking environments, nomads often assist each other in learning the ropes of remote work, with many attempting to make money in "drop-shipping," before moving on to other opportunities. Drop-shipping means establishing a website that sells trinkets, which will be automatically shipped from the distribution center. However, nomads quickly learn that driving traffic to one's website is more difficult than anticipated.

Finding Remote Work

> Middle class knowledge workers soon realize that a corporate career will not give them the possibility to realize themselves and have an impact in the way that they were taught in college. (Arvidsson, 2019, p. 35)

Universities encourage students to major in aspirational career trajectories, though rarely do people land in the profession of their college major. Aspirations are rarely achieved shortly outside of college for this generation, and this leads to paths of exploitation in unpaid internships where gaining experience in one's desired field may become more valued than even earning a salary (E. B. Duffy, 2017). The aspect most valued about employment opportunities for digital nomads is the possibilities for various mobilities, which Schlagwein and Jarrahi (2020) categorize into four areas: administrative mobility (working independently of an organization), spatial mobility (remote location), temporal mobility (when to work), and content mobility (defining one's own work).

Many of the digital nomads had experience working on a very subsistence level, including exchanging labor for lodgings. Haley, originally from the UK, had work a long list of entry-level jobs and enjoyed trading labor for lodgings as she had done for years:

> I've been working since I was 13. Illegally for a while in a grocery store. I escaped to the States, and I went and lived for a year and got a job in Macy's as a perfume sprayer, which is really random. I came back to the U.K. and I worked in lots of different bars, restaurants, in the hospitality realm. Nothing that lasted too long; I was never very happy in anything. I ended up getting a job in fashion, which was really crazy, because it was this high-up position, and it was for a public relations company. I didn't even know what PR meant at the time, but I managed to get the job, and I stayed there for about a year and a half. And then I started traveling. I didn't have money for a few years. I traveled, worked on farms for just food and accommodation. I made a lot of friends through that. There was a husky dog farm in Austria that I stayed in. He would always give me a bit of money to get to my next place, and I really enjoyed the work, so that's kind of how I was managing to get around. I was doing that for about two and a half years I'd say.

Haley had been managing gig work for years before her transition to digital work. Shearmur (2018) seems to be envisioning Haley's experience when he writes:

> As a result of this casualization of labour contracts, workers face intense pressure and competition. They are constantly defending their current gig, as well as preparing the next one. Hence, the workday extends well beyond traditional hours and work is performed in all types of locations (e.g., homes, offices, cafes, parks, and transit). As a consequence, the separation between work and leisure – in terms of time and location – is blurring. (p. 94)

Haley was once scraping by, working under-the-table farm labor in exchanging for food and lodging, always with an eye out for the next gig. When she became a digital nomad, she found work as a digital personal assistant. Later, she developed a business model in which she was recruiting and training other people to become remote personal assistants and developed a de-factor employment agency. Some of the independent contractors she would recruit were based in the Philippines, India, or other countries with English-speaking backgrounds and widespread poverty (P. Taylor, 2010, p. 22). Haley also recruited Westerners to work as personal assistants. This was a similar business model to that developed by Taylor, who was based in Guatemala. She had found remote work, and after her friends asked her how she was able to pull it off, she began a small business in which she sold information on how to find remote work. Taylor shares with me how she got her start:

> I applied to everything under the sun in customer support. I had been a bartender, a lot of volunteering, and I was a teacher, so I know how to make people happy. Even though I didn't have any online experience, I felt like I could give it a go. I did get rejected a lot, but I got accepted to work as a customer success manager. It's an e-mail marketing platform. I worked with them for about a year. That was my first ever remote job with zero experience. That's what kind of led me to develop [my company]. I was getting all of these questions from friends, acquaintances, and people I would meet when I travel. "What do you mean you just work for a European company, but you live here? I don't get it." So, I just started that awareness that it is possible, any old Joe can do it. I was like, "I think I have something here." And multiple people told me that I needed to make a business out of it. So, that's what I did.

Both Haley and Taylor started with their own journey to find employment and then sold their skill at finding such employment to others – thus becoming remote employment coaches. The coaching industry is estimated to be a $2 billion industry, with 53,300 coaches estimated to be operating globally by 2016 (Dunlop, 2017). This profession is unregulated, without required degrees or licensure.

Individuals sell services as a life coach, or specialize in a particular arena, such as romantic life, thus encroach on the professional turf of therapists and psychologists. Coaching is a popular pursuit for nomads, dovetailing with attempts to monetize their websites, Facebook groups, and e-books. This especially overlaps with female-dominated remote work sectors (E. B. Duffy, 2017, p. 35).

Kam and Nate are a long-term couple and co-organizers of the digital nomad conference. While Nate was previously employed in software design and could find freelance work, Kam made less money, as she explains:

> I would say that Nate was definitely making more because he was doing contracts with big Silicon Valley companies. I was probably only making $20,000–$30,000 a year. He was probably making $50,000–$70,000. We were making enough because we were living quite cheaply. In those early nomad days, "I can stay in this place for $10 a night. It's amazing!" And, you eat whatever you can get for a dollar. It's super cheap. I remember people back home saying, "Oh my gosh, you must be so rich to travel." It was very clear to me that as we continued and graduated from just renting rooms from Airbnb and then renting whole apartments and wanting to stay in nicer places, we were working the bare minimum. So, I was like, "We could just work more." And approach half of how much we used to work in L.A. and make tons more and afford more. It would be relatively easy to scale up and afford whatever level of lifestyle we wanted, to a point.

Many of the participants were engaged in female-dominated digital gig work such as social media advertising, marketing, translation, content creation, and writing. The men were often in computer programming, software design, web design, and one was retired from the airlines and living off a pension. Some of the participants were in male-dominated fields such as software design, law, and one was a former Hollywood producer (now coach). Baudrillard (2005) refers to advertising as creating "communicational warmth" (p. 186).

Journalism is an industry being heavily decimated by the transition to digital platforms, where social media content competes for readers, the elevated bankruptcy of city newspapers, and the reduction of full-time staff. Writing Search Engine Optimized (SEO) content for websites is a gig that several of the participants engage in regularly, where they make between $10 and $100 per article. In this context, some journalists now turn to crowdfunding to raise money for their stories (Hunter, 2015). This is a dangerous trajectory for freedom of the press and democracy. Now, click-bait content is written for the sole purpose of gathering eyeballs. Other participants worked as freelance translators, another industry facing intense competition from voice-to-print technology and other translation software quickly putting full-time workers out of business (Kushner, 2013). The translation industry is estimated at $7.3–$13.2 billion USD, with a growth rate between 5% and 7.5% and freelancers account for up to 80% of the industry (Kushner, 2013, p. 1243). Digital nomads' gain currency and legitimacy by widening their social media audience in the hopes of finding corporate sponsors who can offer products in exchange for favorable mentions. In such a world, one's following is equal to one's significant in the social media habitus.

Digital Surveillance

The rise of digital technology is also a rise in digital surveillance. Online platforms employing freelancers include an extensive array of tracking and monitoring work output, performance reviews, and personal data. In Makimoto and Manners (1997) manifesto on digital nomads, they stated: "Governments naturally hate nomads. They are difficult to tax and impossible to control" (p. 48). While governments may have outmoded methods of tracking citizens, private companies fill in the gap with society-wide surveillance techniques. Like companies, digital nomads also enjoy finding ways to evade paying taxes by working outside of their own country, denying they are "working" in the host country. As Wang, Schlagwein, Cecez-Keemanovic, and Cahalane (2019) find in their research, digital nomads typically do not pay taxes in their host country as they travel on tourism visas, thus working in a gray zone of taxation evasion (p. 8). Millennials are less concerned about privacy rights that Generation X, who grew up before the establishment of the internet and its endless tracking mechanisms. Freelancers working on platforms have each of their interaction with customers logged and tracked: respond time, performance, and customer complaints become a part of one's record and can result in loss of future work (Ravenelle, 2019; Rosenblat, 2018). Yet, if there is a problem, there is a lack of customer service support for resolution of negative outcomes. One's data become one's digital value. Digital nomads know this and are quick to gather e-mail addresses for later advertisements of one's services (Fortier, 2001, p. 51). Fortier (2001) warns against such hopes of the digital commons replacing civil society:

> But as the dust settles on the hype of cyberspace, we can see that the benefits of computer networks can barely maintain the former positions of civil society organizations, let alone emancipate work, empower consumers, or democratize the media. (p. 71)

Employment Benefits

Because the participants, like many digital nomads, are freelancers, they often do not have employment benefits, but some may have benefits based on citizenship. Only 13 of the participants have health insurance based on citizenship. Seven participants (primarily Americans) have private health insurance, for which they pay a premium. Only one has travel health insurance. Two state that they do not have health insurance. This lack of health insurance – most prevalent in the United States – points to the weakening benefits provided to younger generations and also points to a youth-oriented assumption that one may rely on one's healthy disposition. Fifteen of the participants had small retirement funds, and two had large retirement funds. Of the two with large funds, these were established during their high-salary full-time employment, and since it ended, they have continued to contribute a small amount to the holdings. Ten had no retirement savings, and the others did not mention it. Overall, we can assume that many young workers, with inflating costs of living, student debt, and rising rents, lack proper savings and retirement. They also do not have access to other benefits that full-time workers often receive (in some countries): paid time off, childcare, educational benefits, dental, vision, family leave, and unemployment pay.

In the United States for 2015 measurements, the poverty threshold for a 65-year-old or older individual was $11,367 per year, and for two people, it rises to $14,326 (Congressional Budget Office (CBO), 2017, p. 8). For Americans working and contributing to Social Security benefits, they will have some minimum income, though hardly adequate for rent and living expenses. The legal age of retirement in Germany has increased to 67 years old, and the pension calculation formula will decrease from 51% of one's net salary to 43% by 2030 (Spiegel Staff, 2012). Most Germans have more than the basic social security to rely on, but this number will surely increase along with the rates of freelance labor. In Australia, the government requires employers to provide workers with a minimum of 9% superannuation. The government promotes a three-pillar approach to retirement funding, including government and individual contributions, with an expected income replacement rate of about 95% when such is achieved. However, the three-pillar approach – requiring government taxation, employer superannuation, and worker voluntary superannuation – is not always achieved, leaving low-income workers with less retirement options. Despite this, Australia offers one of the most comprehensive retirement programs among industrialized nations (Fairhall, 2009). In the UK, under 2018 new rules, the minimum requirement for pension contributions under auto-enrolment will be 8% of a worker's salary, 4% of which will come from the worker (Uren, 2013). Such strong government retirement benefits may promote some retirees to travel, making up a percentage of the digital nomad population, as researched by P. Green (2020), but this age group was not encountered in my research.

Work-Life Balance

Makimoto and Manners (1997) foresaw that one group would have insurmountable difficulties in achieving the digital nomad lifestyle:

> There is one group of people for whom the nomadic lifestyle does not seem to loom – parents. Schools are a geographic tie from which it seems impossible to break free. (p. 162)

While digital nomad proponents, including the participants in this study, always make the argument that it is possible, there are sparse examples – and I was unable to successfully interview one. Those with families may take on other alternative lifestyles, such as downshifting in order to spend more time with children, but constant travel with small children does not seem to be popular (Hamilton & Mail, 2003). Indeed, for full-time workers able to work from home – they face increased difficulties in balancing the duties of work and family life, with each encroaching on the other (Eddleston & Mulki, 2017). Eddleston and Mulki (2017) found disparate outcomes for male and female workers when they had small children – women felt their family and work were more integrated while working from home, whereas men felt it was more of a conflict and distraction. Furthermore, 56% of female remote workers "lamented that their spouse/partner did not respect boundaries between work and family and that they needed to work while at home," yet only 10% of the male workers felt the same (p. 366). Finally, one of the biggest complaints for remote workers is that of feeling lonely and disconnected (Busch, Nash, & Bell, 2011, p. 4).

Conclusion

In the digital nomad promotional literature, freedom of setting one's own schedule is often centered as a significant benefit for this lifestyle. Indeed, Tim Ferriss's book, *The 4-Hour Work Week*, is widely read and is one of the bibles of the movement. However, none of the participants have been able to survive on a four-hour workweek in this study. The majority of the participants had made the leap into the lifestyle before securing a remote job that could sustain them financially. Their search for remote work resulted in entry-level gig work. At least two enterprising individuals made their search into a micro-business, where they sold the job information they found to members of their online communities. The participants were primarily in their mid-20s and, therefore, had completed college and had minimal entry-level work experience, and only a handful had more significant full-time employment history. Working for the platform economy comes with constant surveillance on one's output and interactions with clients, thus pointing to the pressures inherent in such remote labor. As the participants found piecemeal remote work, it did not contribute to their retirement funds nor unemployment protections, so such workers lacked benefits that full-time employees received. Remote work contains a high level of surveillance where each activity that the worker engages is recorded, documented, and becomes a part of their larger record. Such platforms do not have transparent procedures for arbitration or dispute resolutions. Often, when workers receive low reviews, they are simply dropped from the platform without recourse. Remote gig work simply does not provide enough income to support a worker. Work-life balance is difficult for such contingent workers. And for digital nomads, only one participant had a grown child; therefore, childrearing activities are prohibitive for this lifestyle of travel and leisure.

Chapter 4

Bright Sided: Positive Psychology and Its Adaptation to Digital Nomadism

Introduction

Positive thinking has been integrated into all aspects of our culture – from business culture, the media, and, most especially, digital nomadism. Positivity has positioned itself as a very popular theoretical framework. However, as will be shown in Ehrenreich's (2007) work, there is a dark side to positivity. This chapter presents a critique of Positive Psychology (PP) as an academic subdiscipline by overviewing its actual creation since its founder, Martin Seligman, became president of the American Psychological Association (APA) in 1997 and pushed his subdiscipline's agenda within the larger academic discipline of psychology. Critics of PP argue that this framework lends itself to neoliberalism – in which each person becomes solely responsible for their own success in a hypercompetitive global economy favoring the rich. Digital nomadism has adopted this orientation in their fundamental premise that anyone could become a nomad if they work hard enough for it. Therefore, those who did not become successful are at fault for their own failures. Few researchers have taken a critical perspective to the application of PP to the general culture, aside from Barbara Ehrenreich's insights (2007). She tells her own story of how positivity was pushed upon her while she was a cancer patient, where her negative attitude was policed and stigmatized. This chapter overviews what the digital nomads themselves say about how PP infuses with their own personal perspectives on work, leisure, and life.

Founding Positive Psychology

The subfield of "positive psychology," was established in 1997 by Martin Seligman, upon his assent to the presidency position of the APA. During his acceptance speech, he introduced his new concept of focusing on a positive approach to psychology, instead of the pathological and mental illness approach for which psychology was known. By 2000, he and colleague Dr. Csikszentmihalyi published their inaugural paper defining the position of the subfield as one moving

Digital Nomads Living on the Margins:
Remote-Working Laptop Entrepreneurs in the Gig Economy, 45–58

Published under exclusive licence by Emerald Publishing Limited
doi:10.1108/978-1-80071-545-520211005

beyond "humanistic psychologists" (Seligman & Csikszentmihalyi, 2000). In turn, "humanistic psychology" was slowly differentiating itself from the limited model established by Sigmund Freud's psychoanalytic theory and B.F. Skinner behaviorism. Humanistic psychology is associated with the early works of Carl Rogers (1951, 1961, 1980), who focused on the personal developmental process necessary to achieve a more creative and optimistic personality. He also promoted the concept of a client-centered therapy. During the 1960s, Abraham Maslow and colleagues founded the school of "transpersonal psychology," in response to his view that humanistic psychology could not explain all aspects of experience. Maslow (1943) went on to establish his concepts such as the hierarchy of needs, arising from survivalist to self-fulfillment. He was actually the first to use the term "positive psychology" in reference to his research.

Seligman (1972, 1975; Hiroto & Seligman, 1975) started out researching depression during his time at the University of Pennsylvania in 1967. He worked as a graduate student in a laboratory where the experiments required that he give electric shocks to dogs, in order to observe how they responded to stress. From this research, he and fellow researchers developed the concept of "learned helplessness," arguing that the dogs learned to submit to abuse. His later research reversed this, arguing helplessness is the original state, and from there, the dogs had to be taught physically how to jump over the barrier in order to avoid the shock. From then on, the dogs followed suit and continued to avoid the shock. This research led to a working relationship with the US military. He gave a talk in 2002 about learned helplessness at the San Diego Naval Base. In attendance was James Mitchell, a military official who would go on to lead the torture program at Guantanamo Bay. Upon the break of this scandalous connection, Seligman released a statement of objection: "I am grieved and horrified that good science, which has helped so many people overcome depression, may have been used for such bad purposes" (Seligman, 2010; Singal, 2014). However, the APA (2008) did not officially make a statement against torture until 2006 (adopted in 2007), even though individuals within this profession were accused of using their professional knowledge to assist in the use of torture by the military.

Thus, the APA presidency provided Seligman with an opportunity to rebrand his own research trajectory to a much more appetizing – and profitable – subject matter. He had moved on from the laboratory days at University of Pennsylvania. Now, he was the Director of the Penn Positive Psychology Center, in addition to Director of the Master of Applied Positive Psychology (MAPP) program. His books were quickly published: *Authentic Happiness: Using the New Positive Psychology to Realize Your Potential for Lasting Fulfillment* (2002), *Character Strengths and Virtues* (2004), and *Flourish: A Visionary New Understanding of Happiness and Well-Being* (2011). His books were popular: widely reviewed in the press, bought by consumers in bookstores, invited to media interviews, awards and grants earned, and honorary degrees granted. PP was a goldmine. Another lucky connection presented itself: Seligman's mentor had a philanthropic father whose organization granted him millions in funding through the John Templeton Foundation and the Templeton Religion Trust ($3,835,702 in 2014–2018); in addition to other, major grants: the National Philanthropic Trust ($5,647,094 in 2014–2017) and Robert

Wood Johnson Foundation ($4,214,969 in 2011–2018). He has also received funding from the US Army, National Institute of Mental Health, US Department of Education, and the National Science Foundation. His books, talks, seminars, conference calls, keynotes to the world's largest corporations, earn him a premium – in one case, a conference call with hundreds of people in attendance costs each listener $2,000 (Schein, 2018). Schein (2018) says about Seligman's popularity:

> Martin Seligman's greatest achievement has been to create a cure-all that corporate America believes in. If you're in the business of selling ideas, find a way to do the same and you'll never want for clients again.

Indeed, his knowledge can come at a steep price.

Mihaly Csikszentmihalyi, Seligman's co-author, has an extensive research track record in his own right. Dr Csikszentmihalyi coined the term "flow," which he outlined in his first book, *Beyond Boredom and Anxiety: Experiencing Flow in Work and Play* (1975). He defines "flow" as an optimal feeling in which the person is fully immersed in what they are doing in a pleasurable manner, creating intrinsic motivation for the activity, along with a great sense of fulfillment (Csikszentmihalyi, 2014). He uses the example of a painter being so involved in the creation of their artwork that they postpone eating or sleeping.

Seligman also wrote with colleague Christopher Peterson, applying his concept of "character development" to the field of PP (Peterson & Seligman, 2004). This research emphasized the individual character traits associated with "strength," as valorized in Western concepts of individuality and competition. Such concepts reinforced capitalist and neoliberal approaches to enterprise and competition. Such simplistic and jargon-free books were perfect for mass consumption, especially for bulk purchase in the corporate world, where such messages reinforced the idea of the ideal worker as one always improving one's self in order to maximize their productive output for the company.

Critiques of Positive Psychology

Barbara Ehrenreich (2007) begins her critique of Seligman's work by examining one of Seligman's biggest funders – the John Templeton Foundation, in which his good friend is embedded. The foundation positions itself at the intersection of religion and philosophy. It has funded pro-war advertisements, an organization called Let Freedom Ring that activated the evangelical Christian vote for George Bush, and Mitt Romney campaign's National Faith and Values Steering Committee. It has also given an $8 million grant for the creation of the Institute for Research on Unlimited Love, at the National Organization for Marriage (an anti-same-sex marriage political organization). The field of Positive Psychology joins this list of grant-receiving fiscal accomplishments in the portfolio of the John Templeton Foundation.

Ehrenreich (2007) attended the Sixth Annual International Positive Psychology Summit conference and calls the papers presented "the full range from mediocrity to silliness." For example, Ehrenreich states, "For silliness, you couldn't beat a couple of sessions featuring 'coaches' and management consultants using their power points to illustrate how to make corporations more 'positive' and 'strength based.' " Indeed, the intersection between mega-church-style positivity such as that of Joel Osteen and the application of this mental outlook to soldiers, students, and corporate employees demonstrates its widespread appeal. Ehrenreich (2007), with her usual dry wit, argues in her article's subheading: "The right-wing philanthropist is pushing the phony science of positive psychology to numb Americans into smiley-faced acquiescence to the status quo."

Ehrenreich (2009) did not simply base her observations on her one-time conference attendance. She has submerged herself into the world of positive thinking for her book *Bright-Sided: How Positive Thinking Is Undermining America*. It overviews PP in order to examine how very malleable and marketable this mindset was, as it was being utilized in all sorts of American institutions. It had become its own industry:

> The promotion of positive thinking has become a minor industry in its own right, producing an endless flow of books, DVDs, and other products; providing employment for tens of thousands of "life coaches," executive coaches, and motivational speakers ... No doubt the growing financial insecurity of the middle class contributes to the demand for these products. (Ehrenreich, 2009, p. 9)

Before *Bright-Sided*, Ehrenreich (2005) wrote, *Bait and Switch: The (Futile) Pursuit of the American Dream*, for which she conducted ethnographic observation in the field of employment networking, an industry in its own right:

> I attended about a dozen of these networking events and boot camps for white collar job seekers in 2005 and found that the core message was positive thinking: whatever happens to you is a result of your attitude; by overcoming bitterness and converting to a positive or winning attitude, you could attract the job of your dreams. (Ehrenreich, 2009, p. 119)

Ehrenreich (2009) points to the dark side of PP, the threat of what happens if one does not take up this positivity programming:

> The flip side of positivity is thus a harsh insistence on personal responsibility: if your business fails or your job is eliminated, it must be because you didn't try hard enough. (p. 8)

Positive thinking places responsibility upon the individual, and their mental outlook, rather than on institutional constraints and societal inequalities. Poverty and neoliberalism are left unexamined, as are the inherent privileges of the upper-classes, the racialized whites, or the position of men in socio-behavioral patterns and networks. Ehrenreich has taken on covert-identities to gain firsthand experience working in minimum-wage and service sector jobs – such as working as a cleaning maid or a fast-food server – in order to write about poverty in America (Ehrenreich, 1983, 1989, 1990, 2001, 2003, 2005). Her research points out the reasons why America ranks low on the *World Happiness Report* (2020): because the survey-designers tie a sense of security in one's life, a stable outlook for one's future, as key to happiness. Thus, happiness is not pure bliss, as digital nomads may conceive it, but a stoic sense of security in one's physical survival. Thus, the United States, with the highest rates of poverty and insecurity among developed countries, would rank low on such measures.

Ehrenreich is not the only writer to challenge the field of PP. Cabanas and Illouz (2018) wrote *Manufacturing Happy Citizens: How the Science and Industry of Happiness Control Our Lives*:

> The term "happycracy" – the title of the original edition – is here coined to emphasize the particular interest of the book in showing the new coercive strategies, political decisions, management styles, consumption patterns, individual obsessions and emotional hierarchies that, together, with a new notion of citizenship, have emerged in the age of happiness (13) ... At the same time, mindfulness has itself become a lucrative, global industry raking in more than $1 billion a year. (p. 66)

The self-help-style books that employers provide to their employees, to get them into a better mindset, in order to serve the profit motives of the company, are big business. Shifting responsibility from institutional establishments to individual motivation is a boon for capitalist ideology – one's failure is based on their lack of desire, not lack of social safety nets and a living wage. Cabanas and Illouz (2018) agree,

> On this premise, happiness scientists articulate a renewed discourse for the construction of a worker identity that is tightly attached to the workplace, to the new work ethic of capitalism, and to the new power distribution within the labor sphere. (p. 94)

Ultimately, they conclude:

> In the end, we are not given much choice: the science of happiness not only obliges us to be happy, it blames up for not leading more successful and fulfilling lives. (p. 10)

Instead of a value neutral science, as Seligman likes to portend, it becomes a cover for an ideological directive – ignore the material constraints and will yourself to be happy (and rich), and if you fail, then own it as the result of not trying hard enough. It verges on ideological because of precisely its lack of reproducible and scientific measures. Many in the field of psychology, and other social sciences, challenge this orientation for being prescriptive. Focusing on positivity itself, as if negativity could be separated in a neat binary, is in itself a disingenuous orientation, as if human emotions could be more than ephemeral (Folkman & Moskowitz, 2003). Cabanas and Illouz (2018) join others in the psychology field, as we will see shortly, in critiquing positive psychologists for their lack of rigorous methodology in preference for packing pithy truisms:

> Lacking a rigorous and common body of knowledge, these professional underpinned their practice by appealing to a half-baked, eclectic mixture of heterogenous sources, ranging from psychoanalysis and religion to behaviorism, medicine, occultism, neuroscience, conventional oriental wisdom and personal experience. (p. 24)

Kurt Andersen (2017) can explain why this hodgepodge of eclectic sources appeals to Americans – highlighting the role of American exceptionalism – in his book *Fantasyland: How America Went Haywire: A 500-Year History*. By overviewing the unique trajectory of American cultural development and the ways in which this Anglo-settler nation blends together religions (from the newly created to the long established), magical thinking, gold rushes, popular culture, anti-science, and the acceptance that people can believe absolutely anything they choose, we can understand how America often ends up at odds with the rest of the world. His writing demonstrates how such a cultural context could lead to a Trump presidency, for example, reflecting this very American mixture of television, entertainment, pop religion, and anti-intellectualism (Andersen, 2020). Andersen (2020) calls these skilled politicians that can efficiently mine this cultural context "evil geniuses." In their hands, tool such as PP obscures the reality of social inequalities.

Psychologists also have critiques of PP (Cederström, 2017). The subdiscipline of critical psychology challenges the field about identity, racism, ideology, and epistemology (Fernández-Ríos & Vilariño, 2016; Holzman, 2013; Kristjánsson, 2013). P. T. P. Wong and Roy (2017) systematically lay out the general critiques of PP: The elitism inherent in the process of Seligman handpicking other elite, well-known and well-funded colleagues to join the field (to which Csikszentmihalyi affirms in 2003, p. 113); leading to cronyism over peer-review; a narrow citation of the literature; lack of rigorous measuring instruments for complex human emotions; individual over collective emphasis; and, of course, the overemphasis on happiness over other emotions (A. Miller, 2008; Robertson, 2018). Other researchers point to the absence of consideration of the socioeconomic context for individual development (Diener, 2003). Others call out PP for unacknowledged borrowing of concepts from eastern philosophy and Confucianism, while also ignoring Asian cultures (L. Sundararajan, 2005; P. T. P. Wong & Roy, 2017).

One entire issue of *Psychological Inquiry* (2003) was dedicated to systematically responding to Richard Lazarus' (2003) challenge to PP. Campos' (2003) argument is that "physical events do not convey affective meaning in and of themselves," but the cultural process of interpretation is significant (p. 110); humans are goal oriented, and the outcome of pursuing goals is both wins and losses (p. 112); that we may lack control of our emotions, and that we also do not have to latch onto, or make of significance, our emotions, but observe them passing (Buddhism-detachment); and that negative emotions are undivided from the positive, it is a false dichotomy (p. 112). J. H. Harvey and Pauwels (2003) and Busk (2016) point out that many positive character developments and meaning come from trauma and grief, and that death and illness are natural aspects of life which we must adapt, not obscure. This is the same approach that Barbara Ehrenreich (2018) explores in her book *Natural Causes: An Epidemic of Wellness, the Certainty of Dying, and Killing Ourselves to Live Longer*. Other psychologists have critiqued the field for a near complete absence of a racial justice orientation. Rao and Donaldson (2015, p. 275) conducted a systematic content analysis of the academic literature and coded for female participation (overrepresented), but only 1% had a feminist orientation; only 37% included racial demographics of participants (89.9% included whites; 63% included black participants); only 2.8% of the articles discussed the impacts of racial identity and structural racism; and finally, only seven articles, a mere fraction of the total 1,628 articles assessed, included an intersectional analysis of both race and gender. Yen (2010) states that not only is race and ethnicity overlooked in the subdiscipline, but the orientation is decidedly American in culture and would have a hard time adapting especially to eastern cultures. Finally, scholars have critiqued the subdiscipline for not enough forays into humanistic and existentialist psychology to answer correlated questions. There is also a lack of engagement with other disciplines in the humanities and social sciences, outside of some handpicked quotes from classical Greek and Roman philosophers contemplating the significance of human life. McDonald and O'Callaghan (2008) adapt a Foucauldian approach to PP:

> We illustrate how positive psychology deploys mechanisms to devalue, subjugate, and discredit humanistic psychology. It also illustrates how positive psychology privileges particular modes of functioning by classifying and categorizing character strengths and virtues, supporting a neo-liberal economic and political discourse. (p. 127)

Indeed, PP has provided a boon to the corporate workplace, where responsibility for worker sustainment has shifted from full-time employment and benefits to one of being a micro-entrepreneur, selling one's self to new clients each day – equipped with a positive attitude. If companies can replace retirement programs with self-help inspirations books through human resources programming, so much for better for the businesses.

Application to Digital Nomadism

Digital nomads are dreamers – they are pursuing an ideal lifestyle – while going against the expected pathway. They are primed to believe in the possibility of doing something radically different, liberating, or pleasurable. The literature to which digital nomads subscribe is firmly based in the field of PP and entrepreneurialism. Indeed, according to Aroles, Granter, and de Vaujany (2020), while digital nomadism is often associated with an alternative lifestyle, notably minimalism and hedonism, it is increasingly framed in capitalist logics of professionalism. PP has found a thriving home in the corporate world, where companies may have their human resources offices provide free self-help books on positivity to their workforce to raise productivity, over providing a salary raise. At the same time that freedom in the workplace is being touted, the social safety net is being dismantled by reduced workplace benefits as well as state benefits. Pykett and Enright (2016) have studied the ways in which companies have utilized their workplace training programs during the financial crisis of 2008 where they have to do more with less:

> We have argued that workplace training programs have become an important pedagogic site for re-education of "neurocitizens," in this case, workers who have developed psychological self-mastery such that they can manage their own emotional states in ways which are both optimistic and optimizing. Workers' conceptions of personal transformation and growth become closely aligned with the goals of their organization, company and the wider economy. (p. 64)

This perspective is as ubiquitous as the air digital nomads breathe. Their platform work is removed from having a fair grievance procedure for workers, let alone a collective response, such as with a union. Workers must align even more with the corporate goals in order to find their own workplace harmony. Each activity becomes an opportunity to promote one's brand and tap their network. Instagram presents the idealized life one projects and wants others to see. It can be promoting the lifestyle and promoting one's ability to achieve that prized image of a laptop on the beach. Indeed, Instagram posts can even be "branded" and linked to one's corporate sponsor, who provided you with the product just for the public review and advertisement. Some nomads may dream of having companies send them "free" products to review, even as a revenue stream. But one must provide the audience, the new currency in the digital era. Digital nomad conferences and workshop often offer new members such "hacks," of figuring out ways to reduce costs on travel, lodging, and consumption. Ideas such as pet-sitting or reviewing products on one's YouTube channel can be seen as small gigs. The positivity and self-reliance of hacking one's way to freedom is an integral aspect of the digital nomad ideology and lifestyle. One could almost say that you couldn't have this lifestyle without the underlying PP. Digital nomads become salesmen, as interviewee Mel states:

> "Digital Bro-mads" are the douchey, salesmen, hyper-masculine kind of bro-culture. It is definitely overpowering. It's the guy who wakes up, has his bullet coffee, and lifts weights ... That kind of behavior. It is the people who read *The 4-Hour Work Week* and take it a little too literally. Some women can fit in. That's not me, so I could never really understand how they fit in. But the women's

> retreat was the response to that kind of toxic culture. Gemma went to those places and didn't connect with those types of people. She wanted to find more people like her who were more authentic. People seeking something a little bit more real than the seven-figure salary. Having money is the core pursuit of the lifestyle. I think that's the differentiator. The people that are just in it for making money, living super cheaply, and feeling like they're living like kings versus more authentic people.

In this quote, Mel notes the significance of how central both the *4-Hour Work Week* and "bro-mads" are to the nomadic community. This shapes the lifestyle culture and recruitment processes. For Mel, this made her seek out an alternative space, which she found at the women's retreat. Nate, the American co-founder of the conference, agrees with the "bro-mad" assessment and justifies the significance of his conference for diversifying the subculture:

> Just like with any community, there are good and bad players. In the people who promote themselves publicly as digital nomads, it has traditionally skewed much more male-focused. Those are just the people screaming the loudest about selling courses, "crushing it" with 6-figure salaries, and hanging out in co-working spaces in Southeast Asia, being a little bro-ey. That being said, my co-organizers and myself set out to explicitly combat the fact that that is the only narrative. Our conference this year was about 90% women. We aim to have at least 75% women at all times. It is not hard. I was one of our only token guys involved in the conference. I am really happy about that. It doesn't have to be an issue but, just like anything, it can be. If you work in Silicon Valley, there is obviously a very huge bro-culture problem, problems with harassment, and people having their space disrespected. It exists everywhere. It exists in the nomad space. In my community, the people I associate with on a daily basis, the people I associate with in the conference, it's a very healthy gender dynamic.

Nate's employment history and educational background have been within a male-dominated engineering school and a well-known tech firm. He saw firsthand how it impacted approaches to work and education when only one demographic was in the room. A diversity of perspectives and opinions provides strength, Nate feels. His friend, Anna, works as a volunteer at the conference and regularly travels with other nomads from this collective. She speaks of how this attention to gender drew her to the conference and its community. Anna says:

> There is a definite difference in a way that a lot of male nomads are selling the lifestyle. It's like this, "I'm a digital nomad. I can teach you how to do this." So, they're making their money off of being a nomad. It doesn't feel good. Or, there are a lot of – I am

> generalizing a little bit because it's obviously not everyone – people who are developers and will come from those spaces and are in high demand. They already have a leg up. If you're coming from a company in California and Silicon Valley and you're like, "No, it's fine. It's easy. Just quit your job and be a nomad," I don't think that is a fair message to be telling the world. I think people trying to say, "This is easy! This is an easy lifestyle" is a bit of a misconception. Also, it is not as hard as people think, either. It is finding a balance. Between genders, I feel that there are starting to be more spaces for women in the digital nomad world. I know there is a lot of fear from women regarding traveling alone, so that is a barrier sometimes. I think men are just – gender-wise – more confident in being able to go out and explore on their own because they don't have to fear safety in a lot of ways.

Anna points to the ways in white men in particular are prized in Silicon Valley start-ups and feel the freest to travel. Women face discrimination in the tech and start-up industries and feel less free to travel. By targeting women and people of color specifically, it provides networking and business opportunities to a group often marginalized in male-dominated spaces.

The literature that promotes the digital lifestyle relies heavily on PP perspectives; it makes the lifestyle sounds easy, achievable by anyone with enough positive visions of success. Makimoto and Manners (1997) published *Digital Nomad* only one year after Seligman's assent to APA presidency. The e-books, blogs, podcasts, and e-newsletters on digital nomadism are primarily inspirational, with little empirical evidence on specific jobs, where to find them, and the associated salary. Indeed, as we learn from Taylor's micro-enterprise, such material is good enough to sell. With so many in the community creating intellectual or design products for sale, there is no shortage of enterprising self-promoters. Indeed, Hannah calls out con artists in the community that she has encountered:

> I discovered there are a lot of con artists. I'm just going to be really frank. I have gone through the whole process of building a startup and talking to people in the startup community. I found that a lot of people in digital nomad space are not the entrepreneurs they say they are. Like for me, entrepreneurship isn't something that you call yourself, it's something that other people call you. You know what I mean? I found that a lot of the times the people who sustain themselves in digital nomadism are doing so in a very unsustainable way. Like they would be these con artists who do these, I don't know, some marketing courses to help other people become nomads so they can also become con artists.

Several of the participants had their own podcasts and websites where they interviewed other digital nomads and posted the content online. While the interviews were always positive and promotional, rarely did they speak of how much money they actually made, number of clients, retirement savings, or if their partner was the one actually paying the household bills. Leaving out such key information, while at the same time purporting to have a success story that is easy and replicable, is disingenuous. Two of the participants spoke in this highly charged positive manner about their own lifestyle, while obscuring their financial precarity. For example, Elizabeth celebrates her success in jumping into the unknown lifestyle without fear:

> Yeah. I just fuckin' did it. I think the key takeaway is that everything is figure out-able, so if you don't know what you're doing, you can figure it out. The internet is a great place that allows us to work online, but it also allows us to learn anything we could possibly want to learn, even stuff that we don't know that we want to learn. You can figure out anything that you need to figure out. Life is a series of trials and errors. I think that being a digital nomad is that series of trials and errors but at hyper-speed. It's failing faster and probably more consistently, but it's a lot more fun.

Elizabeth was able to rely on her family support to provide her with a flight to Thailand where she had signed up to teach English. However, upon arrival to the Thai village in which she would teach, she quickly lost interest in the endeavor and cut the job short. But she stayed on in Thailand and met digital nomads in the coworking spaces. When I spoke with her, she was engaged in a house-sitting stay in exchange for lodging. She had less than $200 in her bank account. It was usually difficult to have participants definitively state how much money they made in a year, often saying it fluctuates widely. I then ask if they filed taxes and what they put down for the last two years. Most were living on thin margins, paycheck-to-paycheck. Maggie, an American nomad, provides encouraging advice for others who want to travel:

> I think the biggest help for me has just been hanging out with other people who are doing it. I think for a lot of my friends who want to work remotely but feel like it's a pipe dream, that would be my biggest advice: try to find others. A lot of my friends who want to work remotely tell their friends and they say, "That's crazy. That's not possible." I think the biggest thing for me has just been hanging out with other weirdos who are doing it – even just travelers. Even when I was just into couch surfing and I didn't know what digital nomads were, I met a lot of people who worked on the marijuana farms in the summer in the U.S. or picked fruit in Australia or summer camp jobs teaching English and then going somewhere else and teaching English. Stuff like that. Or work exchange, where they didn't get money but had a place to stay.

Maggie was an interesting case, as she was a descendent of a very wealthy and well-known family, raised by a single mother who worked as a nurse, and her father was a well-off and free-spirited man. As a child, she dined with her wealthy grandmother on Sundays, dressed in formal attire, and then lived between the mid-west and California as a high school student. While her grandmother had paid for her college education, she did not mention whether she received further family funding for travels.

Kelly, a co-founder of the conference, points out that their target audience is for those who have been nomadic for one or two years, they did not encourage aspirants or newcomers to attend, in order to avoid the appearance of selling the lifestyle. They were purposefully constructing a community of established nomads who were seeking detailed information on aspects of the lifestyle. The information they discussed included topics such as securing secondary residency in another country or establishing one's business in a particular country. As most aspiring or new nomads may burn out in their first year, by restricting attendance to those who have maintained the lifestyle for enough time to get through the initial hardship, they were able to reach those who would be more committed to a long-term endeavor in the lifestyle. Kelly shares:

> The biggest advice is to not label, or pigeon-hole yourself, into the digital nomad term. A lot of people get hung up: "I need to travel this much. I need to have a carry-on only." Those are all things you figure out along the way. Setting yourself up financially beforehand is important, so you have backup plans. You don't just jump into it and end up stuck in Thailand for whatever reason. Also, just finding your community. Finding the people that you can reach out to or use as mentors in this space. I latched onto my co-organizers. There are some people that latch onto me. I have had a few I have coached through some nomad stuff. Finding that person you connect with and letting them show you the ropes or get through the first few baby steps of nomad life.

Both Kelly and Maggie point to the importance of community for entering into the digital nomad lifestyle successfully and finding friends with whom to travel and engage in leisure pursuits. All of the participants were active in communities, but certainly other nomads have a more solitary existence or integrate more fully into their destination locations. All of the participants read, believed in, and wrote their own positive narrations of entering the lifestyle. By focusing only on the positive of the lifestyle, it by definition ignores the more challenging aspects or the loneliness that nomads often suffer. However, by engaging in the lifestyle narrative, one might also be pushed to be more extreme in an effort of standing out from the crowd or attracting more followers on social media. Mariza warns of the danger of following social media trends, which promote hierarchies based on more extreme travel or leisure behaviors. She says such trends lead to burnout and can sour people on the lifestyle:

> I see in myself, and a lot of new folks, is that they try to do it this lifestyle too hard-core. They have a mental stereotype of what it

> is to be a digital nomad. Saying stuff like, "I've got to carry everything I own on my back. I have to have an Osprey backpack. I have to make a schedule and make sure that I move every 2 weeks. I need to see as much as I can in the next 6 months. Always have a ticket booked somewhere." It's very mentally exhausting. Your identity changes a lot incorporating these different experiences. You need time to process that mentally. I've burnt out. A lot of my friends have burnt out the first few months or year. Then, there's guilt with quitting, too. You're not a sellout if you have a suitcase. I tell them not to stick to a certain image of a nomad. Make it what you want it to be for you.

Gemma, the founder of the women's retreat and Facebook community, still struggles to develop her community and to monetize it. Like many, she and her boyfriend began their nomadic adventure in the coworking spaces of Chiang Mai. She did the gantlet of nomadic jobs, such as drop-shipping (websites sales of gadgets mailed out from a central distributor). Both she and her partner had earned PhDs in chemistry, before deciding a life in the pharmaceutical industry was not for them. Now, her partner Jason writes chemistry abstracts for academic journal articles, at 10 dollars each, while Gemma tries to grow her networking business online:

> Most digital nomads I know work way more than the people I know back home, who have normal jobs. Nomads are building something from scratch; and that takes a lot of time and effort. It is easy to get obsessed; especially if you are building your own business. It's not just the photo of me sitting at the beach with the laptop. That's not the reality, though, for most people. It's hard work. But, if you're willing to learn and put the time in, it's possible. On the one hand, I think everybody can be a digital nomad. On the other hand, it's not true. You have to have certain privileges. I have a UK passport that allows me to travel. If you talk to people who come from Asian countries, African countries, a lot of South American countries, they just don't have that same freedom.

Gemma captures this ambivalence that some nomads express about providing advice to lifestyle aspirants. On the one hand, anyone (with a strong passport, education, and financial resources) can aspire to be nomadic, but in the end, they have to make a living. Selling Facebook ads might only earn a few dollars for each product and many of the nomads are living on poverty wages (by their home countries' standards).

Conclusion

In this chapter, we overview the beginning of the subdiscipline called PP as it was first established by Martin Seligman during his first address as the new president of the APA in 1997 (the same year that *Digital Nomad* was published). Attempting to "re-brand" psychology away from its association with the abnormal and mental illness, he persuaded the field of the importance on focusing on positive emotions and psychological outcomes. This became reduced to the isolation of positive thoughts and outlook in itself, removed from the larger socioeconomic context of one's social position. This field of literature was quickly popularized and spread to the corporate and entrepreneurial world, where the positive outlook easily adapted to the neoliberal orientation of business. Barbara Ehrenreich and other authors have been critical of the field of PP precisely because of its widespread adoption in the world of business. This trickled down to the digital nomad lifestyle literature, which emphasizes hedonism and happiness, positivity, as a central component orienting one's life. In the digital nomad promotional literature, it is not hard to find passages that reflect PP's emphasis on one's personal attitude for their future success. This chapter has attempted to present a broader and more detailed perspective of how PP has developed and spread to most social institutions. The ideology is foundational in the digital nomad aspirational literature.

Chapter 5

Laptops, Sunscreen, Surfboards, and Selfies: Travel, Tourism, and Leisure Practices of the Digital Nomads

Introduction: The Leisure of Travel

This chapter takes a critical approach for understanding leisure, in relation to the digital nomad lifestyle, within the context of the global tourism industry. Caplan (2000) frames the importance of a critical approach for understanding leisure travel:

> Moderns value mobility, especially leisure travel, and many of us take traveling for granted. But if travel is central to modernity, then the critique of travel must be a fundamental priority in contemporary critical practices. In this critical approach to deconstructing something that one engages deeply and cares about, the term travel signifies the multiple aspects of an expanded field including transportation and communications technologies, divisions of labor, and representational practice. (p. 32)

In order to sociologically analyze travel, we must first understand that most migration on earth is involuntary – people are compelled to move because they are pushed out by natural or human-made disasters in their home countries. Thus, the initial adoption of "nomad" for digital nomads erases the historical use of the term, which refers to subsistence shepherding people who migrate seasonally with their animals within a well-defined territory. Kaplan (2002) explains:

> In focusing on the production of postmodern discourses of displacement in modernity, this study calls attention to the continuities and discontinuities between terms such as "travel," "displacement," and "location" as well as between the particularized practices and identities of "exile," "tourist," and "nomad." (p. 161)

Digital Nomads Living on the Margins:
Remote-Working Laptop Entrepreneurs in the Gig Economy, 59–79

Published under exclusive licence by Emerald Publishing Limited
doi:10.1108/978-1-80071-545-520211006

The majority of mass migration is comprised of people fleeing extreme poverty and instability in their home countries – often in postcolonial contexts. Kaplan (2000) contrasts this forced migration against that of tourism, arguing tourism itself reinforces "new versions of hegemonic relations" (p. 63).

This chapter provides a critical context of understanding tourism as the backdrop for the digital nomad lifestyle. This chapter first overviews the earliest travel memories of the participants as they grew up with their families and how these family vacations shaped their interest in travel. This chapter then discusses the destinations favored by nomads. This chapter concludes by discussing how the nomads interact with the local residents of their destination locations and their engagement with language learning.

Tourism as Serious Leisure Consumption

The digital nomad lifestyle is what Robert Stebbins (2001) would call "serious leisure" – a pursuit for which individuals give a significant amount of time and resources. This is in contrast to what Stebbins defines as "casual leisure," an activity requiring little effort or planning, such as watching television or attending a concert. Digital nomadism is a lifestyle requiring a great deal of effort and commitment: challenges from family and friends, unorthodox lifestyle, isolation, lack of community, and the constant strains of traveling. Robert Stebbins (2007) has also applied PP to the discipline of sociology, by defining "positive sociology," as "the study of what people do to organize their lives such that those lives become, in combination, substantially rewarding, satisfying, and fulfilling" (p. xv). While tourists collect souvenirs to display at their office, to signify a vacation once taken, digital nomads produce magazine-ready Instagram feeds of resort beaches but carry little with them in their minimalist backpacks (K. Stein, 2011, p. 303). Digital nomads are still consumers – just of different products – flights and Airbnb apartments. Baudrillard (2007) wonders if this "lack" is fed by

> a kind of fantastic conspicuousness of consumption and abundance, constituted by the multiplication of objects, services and material goods, and this represents something of a fundamental mutation in the ecology of the human species. (Baudrillard, 2007, p. 25)

Nomads refer to their life-changing travel experiences; are they merely consumption? Robert Dunn (2008) offers some insight:

> Through consumerism, the experience of self and other is increasingly framed by the idea that life's meaning is reducible to the purchase, ownership, and use of commodities and what these commodities signify about the person. (p. 8)

Dunn (2008) further suggests that this focus on experience, over objects, and identity-seeking, "through image-based imitation means increased attention to external features of the self, most notably the body and personality" (pp. 180–181). Thus, such consumption may reflect an idealized self-image, using the tropical paradise – and its people – as a mere prop. This quest for authenticity results in a "disjoined, fragmented, of semi-selves" oriented toward influencing or connecting with a multitude of equally fragmented others (Guignon, 2004, p. 126).

Early Travel Experiences With Family

In *Distinction*, Pierre Bourdieu (1984) defines the social role of "taste cultures," how we come to formulate a particular consumptive practice, and how such taste distinctions are cultivated by our culture, social class, and families. Bourdieu (1984) states:

> Every material inheritance is, strictly speaking, also a cultural inheritance. Family heirlooms not only bear material witness to the age and continuity of the lineage and so consecrates its social identity, which is inseparable from permanence over time; they also contribute in a practical way to its spiritual reproduction, that is, to transmitting the values, virtues and competences which are the basis of legitimate membership in bourgeois dynasties. (p. 77)

Bourdieu focuses on class distinctions, the ways in which the wealthy keep ahead of the masses in their consumptive practices, quickly dropping items that become mass marketed. As children, we have our first exposure (or not) to travel with our family, taking in their perspectives. Structurally, we are impacted by our national paid leave policies. According to the International Labor Organization (ILO, 2013), 96% of all countries provided a minimum period of annual paid leave (vacation, family leave, and sick days). A sizable number of countries (43%) legislate to provide citizens with a minimum of 20 days or more of paid time off (p. 16). Less than 4% of all countries do not have a universal statutory minimum amount of annual leave. These countries include Tonga, Palau, Naru, Micronesia, the Marshall Islands, Kiribati, and the United States. Examining global regions, in Africa, 68% of countries offer 15–23 paid days of annual leaves, and another 22% provide 24 days (ILO, 2013, p. 17). In Asia and the Pacific, 54% of countries offer less than 14 days of leave. In the Americas and Caribbean, the majority of countries (88%) offer 10–23 days, with 66% of countries providing 10–14 days. In the Middle East, 40% of countries offer 20–25 days off, while another 40% offer 10–19 days, and 20% offer more than 26 days of paid leave (ILO, 2013, p. 17).

Europe provides the most paid leave for citizens holding full-time employment, with 94% offered more than 20 days of paid leave, and no European countries provide less than 10 paid days (ILO, 2013, p. 17). Europeans are positioned most favorably to enjoy paid vacation. (This applies to full-time workers, not short term.) Americans as the least. William Chalmers (2013) points out in his book *America's Vacation Deficit Disorder: Who Stole your Vacation?* that Americans do not take many vacations compared to their counterparts in other industrialized nations. Chalmers does not only refer to the national policy that places Americans in the 4% of global countries with no paid leave. He argues that the impact of this policy has infected the mentality of Americans toward holidays. They simply cannot afford it. If they do save up all year for their two weeks of vacation, they overwhelmingly purchase packaged tours or all-inclusive resort stays (Blackshaw, 2017, p. 83). George Ritzer's (2012) concept of McDonaldization – mass production and standardization of goods and services – can be applied to the package holiday, offering few surprises, regardless of location. Two of the American participants explicitly mentioned such packaged holidays. Disney theme parks are the holy grail for childhood travel. Marcella shares:

> When I was very little, we all went to Yosemite [National Park]. We would go to Disneyland a lot, as it is a 7-hour drive, mostly with my mom. We would hike with my dad. In high school, I did go on a trip to the south to trace the civil rights movement. We met a lot of civil rights leaders: people who met Dr. King. We went to a lot of historical sites. That was about 10 days. I went to some new states that I had not been to and saw where history happened. Those were my first kinds of traveling experiences. Not as a family, though, and not out of the country.

Marcella had a range of travel experiences, far beyond Disney World, to include educational trips, and nature adventures, with each parent taking the lead in their preferred travel. Marcella's parents were both highly paid professionals, and she was provided with a rich educational life. Indeed, when I met her, she was the only current college student of the aspiring digital nomads. She has already traveled extensively at age 22, and the women's retreat was just one of her many current adventures. Kelly shares a similar story:

> We traveled a little bit. We did Disneyland. Went to Mexico a lot for Christmas. I went through the States on the west coast quite a bit. When I was 16, I went to Germany with my grandparents for a month. My brother and I went with them and drove all across Germany and met a whole bunch of relatives. My dad's more of a resort traveler. My mom is a little bit more adventurous, I guess, in the world.

Some participants have an international and diasporic family that provided another pathway for early travel. Mirtha is from the Dominican Republic and has just been granted a Spanish passport. During her childhood, she remembers a trip to New York City, because her father was able to acquire a tourist visa. They had only a modest trip planned to visit her father's friend and to see the city. Leisure trips for the family were rare, she shares:

> My parents would travel, but just to work. That's what it meant to travel abroad. It was something they would do to get some money, to provide for us. It was for holidays. Oh, no. I remember one time

> that we spent two months in New York City. It was because my father got us a tourist visa (the children and my mom) and, if you don't use it, they're going to take it away from you. So, I spent a summer there. I remember the first time I ever traveled; I was 10 years old. I spent 2 months in New York City. We were just at a friend's house. We didn't do much. We were just there.

But this was a significant shaping experience for Mirtha. She pursued opportunities to travel abroad and end up living, and working, in Spain. Now, she wanted to travel beyond Spain. Her older boyfriend was less interested. Mirtha was one of the few black, or Afro-Caribbean, participants, standing out among the white racial homogeneity of digital nomad spaces. Whites who travel internationally for leisure are granted more esteem, than immigrant families traveling among their diasporic connections. Hannah had an international childhood, transitioning between different cultures, languages, countries, and family members. Hannah recalls:

> I grew up in quite a few cities. I've been traveling since I was really young due to my parents' situation with work. My dad was a researcher. He actually immigrated to New York when I was little, so I've been living on and off with both my parents, and also with my grandparents, back in China. They had to send me back a couple times just because we didn't have enough finances to afford living in the states and in Canada. I grew up in a rural area in China for a while. I received some education in a Chinese city. And then went to grade school in New York and also in Canada.

Hannah developed rich cultural perspectives living between three nations as a small child. She became a tech worker, with a background in start-ups, one of which she co-created and sold for a profit. This has led her to work on innovative technological products targeted at markets in developing nations. She has lived and worked in eastern Africa on a phone app addressing the issue of food delivery. She was a speaker at the conference and was one of the few to call out digital nomads on their white and Western racial privileges. Her multicultural background, and employment history in tech and start-up industries, provided her with great insight into how different cultures and industries intersect. Her work rooted her in a location for months at a time, engaging deeply with community members.

Liza grew up in the UK, but her father was usually at sea. Her family spent little time with her seafaring father:

> Weirdly, I think it was more my father going to sea, which affected me. He used to spend three months at sea, then a month at home. He would return to the sea for another three months. Sometimes, it was six months. That was the pattern. Leaving has been a constant in our house. We are always emigrating, and returning, or

> going to sea. We were always picking him up at ports, mostly in the UK, sometimes to the Netherlands. Work involves travel. He was always on his way to Nigeria or coming back from Nigeria. My mother's family is Polish and Russian-Jewish, my father's family is Irish Catholic, there is a diaspora on both sides. The Irish diaspora is probably more pronounced. My whole family is scattered to the wind. There was always this feeling that people move. Staying in one place seemed a bit odd to me.

Liza continued this lifestyle throughout her adult life. She worked on Hollywood productions, which would land her in a specific location for months at a time. Now that she is working her own consulting business, she would like to stay rooted and near her aging father:

> The term I use is location independent. I don't move all the time. At the moment, I'm moving quite a lot. Essentially, I like to live in maybe 2 or 3 places a year. I've been completely nomadic for about 4 years. For the nature of what I'm doing in my business, it's not convenient to be living like this but, until I can live full-time in the U.S., this is the next best option. I think the difference is that nomads are working so they can travel. I am finding that I am going to places to work. I have no interest in traveling there at the moment. I just want to sit very still with good internet and grow my business. I don't want to be kayaking or hiking. That's not what I'm there for.

Some of the participants had parents with conflicting perspectives on travel. Some had one parent more interested in travel than the other; or who were more supportive of their own travel, than the other parent. Chelse witnessed her parents differing opinion on travel, which resulted in one giving up the dream of their own travel:

> My mom was always way more adventurous than my dad. My dad is warming up, but he is West Virginia through and through. He doesn't care to learn about the outside world, at all. He is in his bubble. That's his attitude. I think my mom secretly always wanted to be more adventurous. It's hard, I guess. It wasn't that she's in a patriarchy – but, she probably felt like she couldn't travel unless dad wanted to travel.

Chelse points out the power differential by mentioning the word "patriarchy," where the men in the family are able to assume a leadership position. She invokes the image of the southern white male when she comments, "West Virginia through and through." She implies in her statement that her father is, of course, not demanding that his wife not travel. But that the wife decides not to travel alone, without her husband, expresses this agreed upon dynamic that does not require any force. The digital nomads in couples were often navigated through locations by the male partner, as he had other ranking statuses in the relationship, such as being the higher income earner. For Kam, the conference co-organizer, she grew up in the United States and took the usual Disney trips and visited family in Maine. Echoing Marcella's emphasis on educational travel, and Maggie's mother's attempts to make her travels educational, Kam also had a mother that stressed visiting educational landmarks during their travels:

> My mom always made sure that we had good experiences. She was an art teacher. During the good years, because my dad was a traveling salesman, he had airlines points, we would fly to visit family in Maine. One year we went to Disneyworld. One year we went to the Caribbean. But, even during years where money was tight, my mom would make sure that we took a road trip to the beach or some colonial town up and down the east coast. My mom is a big believer in educational travel.

This illustrates the mother's increased attention to matters of creating educational opportunities out of travel experiences. In Maggie's case, her mother's similar desire to educate her children through travel was directly credited for Maggie's own wanderlust:

> She loved it. She did. It is interesting because, now, she is always flitting around everywhere. I am like, "Mom, you're as spacey as I am in terms of how much you travel!" She's, like, "Yeah. Don't you remember? That's why I was always taking you on road trips." I'm like, yeah, I guess that makes sense. She was always trying to educate us and get us out of the house for the summers. It was also her drive and her desire.

Finally, several of the participants mentioned the influence of grandparents on their lives. Some were raised by grandparents or spent a great deal of time with them in their childhood. Elizabeth was influenced by the frequent travel she witnessed her grandparents engage in:

> If it wasn't for my grandparents, I probably wouldn't have traveled. They were always taking trips, planning trips, and wanting to go somewhere new. It seemed just like something that you do. It wasn't like you saved up for two years to go to an all-inclusive resort. I think the attitude that a lot of people have is different: where you save up and your trip is a respite from the world. You go and sit on a beach to get away from work and e-mails and jobs. I think I had a different attitude, and that's probably because of them.

Early travel experience and witnessing the travel of family members worked to normalize the practice for the nomads. It was something people did, to quote

Elizabeth. So, this became an option when the participants grew older, graduated from college, and realized that making enough money was going to be a challenge. They also faced being pushed out of expensive cities, regions, and even the country itself. For Anna, who had an elite education and spoke several languages, she still only achieved entry-level employment opportunities in New York City. But rent was sky high. Anna recalls:

> Rent in New York City is pretty awful. For the most part I've lived with roommates, and the last, like what, four, five, almost six years I was in New York I was living in Queens, because the rent had gotten really expensive in Manhattan. Yeah, so rent was a lot. I paid a lot more for my rent in New York City.

For Alexis, a mixed-race Asian and white lawyer who had previously held full-time employment with major firms in the United States, Asia, and Hong Kong, she finds herself currently living with her parents in Florida in order to save money, especially considering her roller coaster salary that makes it difficult to financially plan ahead:

> My home base is in Florida. I live with my parents right now. Honestly, I was just like, "I want to save as much money as I can this year." Once this other job hits, then I'm going to probably, I don't know. I could be traveling so much next year; it may not make sense for me to be paying rent anywhere. To be honest, this is what I've done with my location independence. I've been able to put away a lot of money. I'm fortunate enough that my parents are willing and able and healthy enough to bring me back in and welcome the prodigal daughter back home after so many years abroad. I know it's not orthodox. This is not what a typical digital nomad does, but it's an option that location independence can give people.

Thus, the familiarity with travel and the sense of being financially pushed from one's hometown often work as motivators to get digital nomads on the road initially.

Chiang Mai, Thailand – Ground Zero for Digital Nomads

Chiang Mai, Thailand, is the current favorite location for digital nomads to gather and get their start in the lifestyle. With affordable living, tropical weather, friendly locals, and many coworking spaces in which to work and meet other nomads, it is the most mentioned place where the participants first arrived and met others in the subculture. Marta, a nomad from Poland, explains:

> I think because it is an easy location for nomads. Southeast Asia, in general, is inexpensive compared to western countries. So, that

> is first. It is inexpensive. It is easy to start. It fits many criteria that digital nomads need: inexpensive, because you don't have much money starting out, and strong Wi-Fi (this is very important). Asia has much better Wi-Fi than all the U.S. and most of Europe. Cost of living, proper Wi-Fi, and it's warm. This is why we travel. Most of us want to go to places that are exotic. Thailand is one of the dream countries that you want to go for holidays, so this would be a dream place to go. It's warm. There is a jungle. You can see islands. There are beautiful mountains in Chiang Mai. Also, it has co-working spaces, but I think that is just secondary. I think it just became that. They have very good co-working spaces with very good conditions for work. It is easy to get by. You can go for lunch and just eat outside. You don't have to cook. The food is amazing, and it is very cheap. It is from the street so you can socialize during your meals. You don't have to worry about things like cooking. Accommodation is inexpensive and it is easy to get short-term leases for a low price.

Marta provided a profound sociological insight into the context of digital nomads in Thailand. As we can see in this passage, it is all about the cost and the hospitality – but nothing of the culture, the people, the language, food, and connection to the actual nation. It is a generic Southeast Asian country. However, Marta reveals more insight into the geo-political situation of nomads in Thailand. She attempts to differentiate nomads from regular tourists, who she portrays as drinking and being disrespectful to the local culture. In the next passage, Marta delves further into the politics of categorizing remote workers, visa requirements, and how digital nomads attempt to evade such regulations:

> We all use tourist visas. We are not working there. We are working for our countries. In Thailand, we are tourists. It is a grey area. The Thai government mixed us with backpackers. In Thailand, many tourists are disrespectful to the culture, but the country lives off tourism, so they tolerate white tourists. When we started, they did not see the difference between nomads that actually make money and have money [and backpackers]. We don't tie up people's jobs, and we spend money there. So, that's basically the perfect situation. In most cases, we are also more respectful because we are people who are trying to build careers. We are not on a year holiday to get drunk. So, the Thai government tended to change laws about tourist visa every few months. We read an article about the co-working space we go to. People were working when the military came. They put everybody on the floor and told everyone they needed to see their passports and their visas. Many people didn't have passports and visas on them. They had them in the hotel, so they were taken to prison. They assumed they were illegally working. The co-working space manager was supporting

> them, bringing them food and stuff. Then, they let them go after a few hours. But the Thai government kept changing the visa situation. For example, being from Europe, you can get a three-months tourist visa. That's the longest one. So, after 3 months, you have to leave. So, what you do is go to a different country and then you go back and get a three-month visa again. So, you do these runs to Laos, to Vietnam. Everybody does visa runs. What happens sometimes, is that you leave your stuff, you go, and then they don't let you in again. It happened to a few friends. Because technically, you should not do this. So, that's a fight between digital nomads and the Thai government, especially since the King died. Now, I think it is going to be more complicated because the military is in charge in Thailand now. The military is very strict. From what I understand, the King was making it more supportive for foreigners. I think, now that he is gone, it may be more difficult. So, that is one reason I would not want to stay there long-term. I don't feel welcome in the way that I have to fight with the government. Whereas, in Spain, I get residency and I get multiple benefits. They see that I am not taking jobs away. Quite the opposite.

She attempts to differentiate the working regulations – which indeed become a gray area when one is paying taxes and supposedly "working," in one country, but is actually working in a location where they have only a tourist visa. Digital nomads are notorious for trying to avoid taxes (Lai, 2020). Often, nomadic conferences will have panel discussions on avoiding taxes or how to register in other locations. The United States and Eritrea are the only countries on earth that charge citizens taxes, no matter where they reside and work in the globe (Lai, 2020). Other countries base it on time spent in country, usually 183 days of the year. Some countries, most notable Estonia, is actually trying to lure digital nomads with a visa specifically for remote workers to stay for up to a year. Other Eastern European countries and even poor American southern states have recruitment lures for remote workers (Lai, 2020). However, this mindset of avoiding taxes demonstrates the digital nomad mindset of avoiding commitments or responsibilities to their temporary locations. They focus on the money they spend in locations but ignore the resources they use in locations and how this impacts local communities. Marta also discusses the impact of living under a military dictatorship in Thailand but focuses exclusively on how it impacts tourists, rather than local people. Marta continues:

> In Chiang Mai, for example, at midnight they stop selling alcohol because of prohibition. You kind of remember the military then. But you don't see them. You know they're there. They stopped us a few times. It's actually police. It's not military. It just looked terrifying when you drive on a scooter. You have to bribe them to let you go. It's a very corrupt place. But you feel safe there. I know it doesn't make sense; but you really feel safe. You would not see

> on the streets of Chiang Mai anything. Like, in the middle of the night, you would not see drunk people. You would not see drugs selling. It is probably there somewhere but you really don't see it. I felt absolutely safe to walk on the streets during the night, except for cockroaches and rats because I don't like them, but people are friendly, nice, polite, and always sober, which is not always the case where I grew up in Poland. You feel safe even though the military is there. I think the assumption would be that they will not hurt you. Military are actually making people behave.

Marta's statement reflects the ambivalence, lack of knowledge on local politics, and focuses on how Westerns are being treated, without a mention of how living under a military dictatorship impacts local residents who do not have the privilege of a strong passport to travel to places which the Europeans have easy access. That Thailand appeases tourists for their financial revenue places them in a position of power in relation to the local community. Marta points to the contributions digital nomads make to the local economy when they spend their money inside the country. This also contributes to the rising prices in tourist centers, and this impacts what locals can buy and where they can live. While accommodations are cheap for Europeans, they are increasingly expensive for the local community.

Marta is not the only nomad who judges a location based entirely on the leisure opportunities offered to Westerners without a mention of local residents. American interviewee Chelse had also started her nomadic lifestyle in Chiang Mai and frames it as an entirely leisurely experience:

> I really like Chiang Mai. I think it's a great stepping-stone if you're starting this kind of life. I recommend it 100%. I'm not really sure you would get the same out of it if you started in Budapest, or Las Palmas, or Barcelona. I think Chiang Mai is a really great place to dip your toes in the lifestyle. I liked working from there, too. I found that, with the time difference, I could do whatever I wanted during the day. I could explore. I could sleep in. I could have a life and then come home and work at night. I feel like when you're on an American time schedule, as soon as you wake up, you have to start working. And what kind of life is that? That's not fun.

Chelse and Canadian participant Elizabeth are both younger nomads, not long out of college, and still happy to work at night and spend the day exploring. Chiang Mai is especially appealing to younger travelers, those with less disposable income, and those attracted to countries that centralize the tourist economy and appease tourist behaviors. Elizabeth speaks of location selection based solely on leisure and affordability:

> I spent a year in southeast Asia. I didn't want to go anywhere cold. Korea is expensive. So, I was in Thailand for the majority. I was in Cambodia for about six weeks. I was in Vietnam for two months.

> I was in Malaysia for two weeks. I was in Sri Lanka for two weeks. I was in Singapore for a week. I was in Bali for two months. Then, I went to Australia. I think I was there for about two months. Then, I went to Paris for a week, England for 3 weeks, and then home [Canada] for a month. Then, I was in Spain for a month. Now I'm in Scotland [house sitting].

Nomads have similar travel itineraries as Elizabeth. Southeast Asia is the favored location and anywhere more expensive will result in a short stay. With little money, younger, and with less working experience, they can still have some power and control over their lives while living in locations where a millennial allowance can still pay the rent. At the time of our interview, Elizabeth only had $200 in her bank account. She was house-sitting for free lodging in Scotland. But she was unsure of her next step or how she would afford it. Family funding was always a possibility if things became too desperate for her. Fewer nomads were interested in locations in South America, with notable hot spot locations such as Medellín, Colombia. Few of the participants had traveled to the African continent and then only to South Africa, Morocco, and Kenya.

Interactions With Local Residents

Urry and Larsen (2011) define mass tourists in this manner:

> Isolated from the host environment and the local people, mass tourists travel in guided groups and find pleasure in inauthentic contrived attractions, gullibly enjoying "pseudo-events" and disregarding the "real" world outside. As a result, tourist entrepreneurs and the indigenous populations are induced to produce ever more extravagant displays for gullible observers who are thereby further removed from local people. (p. 290)

Digital nomads do position themselves as superior to tourists. Digital nomads dedicate their lives to travel and aspire to be a 100% remote worker and full-time traveler. Yet, their selection of destination locations overlaps greatly with mass tourists: Southeast Asia, Spain, and Greece. While none of the nomads reported staying in all-inclusive resort hotels, none of them reported finding local apartments through local people and engaging with locals outside of tourist pathways. For their commitment to long-term travel, few integrate into local life. Rather, they chose Western-style accommodations, such as Airbnb apartments in neighborhoods welcoming to expats.

Gmelch (2012) writes about Caribbean service workers in the tourist industry, who's primary question is: "How can they come so far and know so little about us?" (p. 212). Is one's home country nothing more than a generic beach landscape backdrop for the visitor's selfies? In Marta's long quotes above, we can guess that her knowledge of the sociopolitical Thai context is quite limited. As we see in their explanation of why certain locations are chosen, it is for generic consumption and services provided; little about the unique cultural heritage of a given country. Understanding this, locals are less resistant to portraying stereotypical indigeneity. For example, on tourist pathways in Peru, such as Machu Picchu, local women and children perform indigeneity, in exchange for tourist dollars. The women who dress in elaborate historical costumes are referred to as "sácamefotos" ("take my picture") and approach tourists to pay to take pictures with them (Ypeij, 2012). Such performances happen in Chiapas, Mexico, around Zapatista-related tourism as well in locations across the globe in which indigenous populations are involved in the tourism industry (Babb, 2012). In tourist economies, where a large percentage of the population works in service industries, their livelihood is closely intertwined with creating a welcoming environment for Westerners. Beggars and homeless people may need to be transported out of sight (Alexander, 2005, p. 56). Urry and Larsen (2011) write of the "smile and positive body language more broadly signal the power of the tourist gaze in orchestrating service encounters" (loc. 1656). Alexander (2005) points out that tourists are unaware of how the locals perceive them – even if they may be seething with resentment. Thailand had been instrumental in marketing its friendliness abroad (Alexander, 2005, p. 83). When Marta did not mention the Thai people, I asked her specifically how she thinks Thais may be impacted by digital nomads or tourism, specifically on the topic of housing:

> In general, digital nomads would not stay very long-term. The apartments we rent are mostly short-term. Apartments locals rent are mostly long-term, so I don't think it is exactly the same. I think we raise prices for short-term rentals. It is possible that, long-term, we raise prices in general because we come from countries where currencies are stronger so we can pay more, and we are okay with that. So, in the long-term, I can understand how that could destroy the economy for locals. The truth is that, in Chiang Mai, most people are not really friends with Thai people because Thai people keep their distance. So, the friends you make in Chiang Mai, are mostly foreigners. Also, Thai people are very polite and very friendly, but that comes from their culture. That does not mean they like you. So, many people misunderstand that. They misunderstand their smiles.

Marta has some insight when she says that Thai people may not like Westerners but attributes it to a polite culture, rather than financial dependence and outright governmental pressures in support of the industry. Marta also conceives of the short-term and long-term housing as distinct, rather than how long-term housing may be converted into short-term holiday stays in order to maximize profits. Similarly, when I asked Gemma, founder of the digital nomad women's retreat, about meeting locals, she compared Spain to Chiang Mai, and how locals did not enter spaces she occupies and, therefore, did not engage with them. She does acknowledge how locals may be priced out of the places she spends her time:

> Las Palmas, more, yes, we know Spanish people. The difference, I would say that in places like Spain or Las Palmas, in a lot of the co-working spaces, there are local people working there. So, you know, you'll meet Spanish people working at the co-working space and people working from around the world. In Chiang Mai, that's not really the case. Because paying a hundred dollars for a co-working space for a month is a lot of money for a lot of Thai people. So, we did meet a few locals but not that many, and mainly through other people. One is the husband of a friend we met traveling in Costa Rica. Long story. But, it's not that easy to meet locals there.

Relations With Local Residents

Jason is Gemma's partner; she is quoted above. They are one of the few couples traveling together. They also got their start in Chiang Mai, but they are currently spending more time in Las Palmas, Spain, a traditional tourist location for British tourists, as they both are. Both of them mention price differentials for British and Thai people. Gemma mentions it as a barrier between Westerners and locals. Jason downplays the impact digital nomads have on the Thai economy:

> From what I've heard, prices are slowly rising in Thailand, but not to a great degree. To me, it seems like there are a lot of people doing this. We go out and meet people, work in the spaces where they work. So, it's like, "There is a ton of people." But, certainly, in the south of Spain, digital nomads aren't even a drop in the ocean in terms of tourism. In Chiang Mai, I think the impact is relatively small. A lot of nomads live quite cheaply; so, they aren't necessarily spending as much as a tourist. I never earned my money in a country I'm staying in, so, essentially, my being there is a plus for them. Everything is money coming from outside Thailand, for example, and being spent in Thailand.

Here Jason is making a distinction between digital nomads and tourists and then downplaying the impact digital nomads have on the rising prices, while at the same time stating that they are contributing in consumer spending, providing income for the country. Indeed, tourism is nearly 12% of the economy with a record-breaking 35 million tourists in 2017 alone (Thakral & Sriring, 2018). For years, the tourism industry has been attracting explosive growth – only to be absolutely shuttered by the COVID-19 pandemic. Other sectors are not facing such high growth, placing even more importance upon tourism nationally. Basically, nomads want to take credit for contributing to the economy through consumption and yet avoid paying taxes nor admitting to their place in rising housing costs that disproportionately impacts local Thai people. They point to the friendly smiles of the locals and how they have warm conversations with them in their favorite restaurants, and yet spend most of their time behind the paywall of the coworking spaces. Nomad Anna wrestles with the behavior of tourists and, yet, tried to position herself in a different category:

> Most nomads have traveled to places where their money goes further. There are going to be certain things that you don't experience because you have plenty of money in this context. You're working, so you have limited time to engage with the culture. But it's good to learn a little bit of the language, to respect cultural tradition. Like I've seen people be really disrespectful, like wearing shorts to temples in town. Or getting angry because a local Indonesian wouldn't let them into a temple when they are wearing booty shorts. How would you feel if someone came to your church and did that? You'd be really pissed off, like don't do it. Ideally, learning about the culture, to be able to give back in some way. And that doesn't necessarily mean throwing money at a problem, but you know, engaging with people. Even if it's just the people at the local café where you work, like learning a little bit about them, learning a little bit about their life, maybe introducing them to a new concept, a new experience. Like I had become friendly with the people at the café I work at most of the time in Columbia, and they remembered me when I came back. I had been here before, in April.

Often when asking the nomads about their relationship with local people, their primary stories revolve around friendly restaurant or café workers whom they visit with regularly. Anna reduces the call for responsibility of inequalities from "throwing money at a problem" to "engaging with people," even if that is just becoming "friendly with the people at the café." This is a service relationship, where the employee or café owner has a financial incentive to have the digital nomad provide return business and feel welcome. It is difficult to assess one's friendship outside of this financial transaction, unless one is entering into that person's private life outside of the commerce transaction. But this story was repeated. Nate, the conference co-organizer, also mentions the café relationship. In relation to his conference organizing, he is engaging with local businesses in deeper transactional manners, but it still remains primarily a business transaction for which the nomads are qualifying as friendships. Nate offers:

> We try to [meet locals]. Some places, we are far more successful than others. Organizing our conference requires interaction with local businesses. You have to form these partnerships. Wherever we go, we tend to frequent a couple of different cafes. Whatever neighborhood you're in, you know there's going to be the one café that has the good coffee or the nice corner booth with a power

> outlet. Inevitably, we'll go there a bunch, and will become friends with the people who own it. We do form these smaller personal relationships.

Nomad Mel blames her lack of connection with locals on being shy and her dread of approaching strangers to chat. She only points to service transactions when pointing to interactions with locals, not deeper connection:

> I'm a shy traveler. It's hard for me to go up to a local and chat. We did a few things, like cooking classes, while we were there. There was a little bit of a language piece in the cooking class. We learned a few words, so we could go to the market and buy our own food – the ingredients – and put the ingredients into a local dish. We would try to go to local restaurants and things like that, the smaller restaurants that were a little bit less touristy. In terms of really feeling like you were immersed into a culture, that wasn't the vibe there, which is just so western, right? It feels a little bit arrogant to be that kind of person in that country.

In contrast, what might a connected relationship with locals look like? Hannah, who grew up between Canada, China, and the United States, works with start-up companies that specifically work with local communities around the globe, including Africa and Asia, where she has spent a great deal of time as a traveler. She has the opposite experience of most of the nomads – she did not spend time in digital nomad spaces and worked on a deep level with local communities, often living among them for months at a time. Hannah states:

> I actually didn't make a digital nomad friend until I returned to Canada. Throughout my entire trip during that year I was pretty much only living with locals and bonding with locals and doing activities with locals and taking on projects, so I was busy with stuff on the ground. And I didn't really look into people who are living the same lifestyle. I just did not have a need to interact with other digital nomads. But I found out through some mutual connections in Chiang Mai that there's all these hubs for people who want to do startups. And I was interested in startups, so I went and visited some of these offices and checked out what people were doing. I was like, "Okay, that's cool, that exists."

Hannah is the only nomad who was in Chiang Mai and not spending the majority of her time in coworking spaces but only saw them briefly. She works on phone applications and software that attempts to address social needs in developing countries. Therefore, she works closely with local communities and has to really listen and get to know their patterned behavior, in order to design a product that locals would actually find useful. Not until she was back in her native country of Canada, did she run into other digital nomads such as herself.

Language Barriers

Jason points to the difficulty of learning a language if one is only in the country for a few weeks. He and Gemma had spent many weeks in Thailand but did not learn more than several words. However, they had spent nearly a year in Las Palmas, Spain, and also did not learn more than a few food items in Spanish. Jason shares:

> It's tough, especially when you're only there for maybe 4–8 weeks. I understand. It's tough to get a local interested in someone who is going to be there for two months and then taking off again. Like most digital nomads, I'm probably not great at trying to integrate or trying to make friends with locals. Sometimes, it's the language barrier and sometimes it's the barrier that you're a temporary person there. Why would they be interested? It goes both ways. We could probably do more but, at the same time, we're prevented by some things. Generally, co-working spaces are really good, particularly in Gran Canaria. Just this past year, it's been a real hub for us in terms of meeting people. The city we live in is quite local. It's quite Spanish and our Spanish is relatively bad. There are a lot of people who don't speak English which, in this part of Spain, is quite unusual. It's harder to meet people. So, yeah, the majority of our friends are nomads wherever we go, pretty much. Or friends of friends.

Jason talks about their brief attempts at language learning but admits that their lack of interaction with Thai and Spanish speakers outside of service relationships makes it unnecessary. He can order food in Spanish, but he cannot hold a conversation. Jason elaborates further:

> In places like Thailand, we just didn't even try. We didn't really plan to stay in Thailand as long as we did; and we certainly didn't have the stamina to try and learn the language because it's so just complex for our western tongues. We have a friend who is married to a Thai guy, who was banging her head against a brick wall with that. We should be doing better with Spanish. We've been in a lot of Spanish-speaking countries for a long time. We've taken some lessons. Some were okay. Some were terrible. But again, part of the reason we haven't learned Spanish better in the last year is because we didn't really plan to be there. We'd planned to be there 3 months. We booked some Spanish lessons. They were terrible so we quit halfway through. We thought, "Well, we'll be leaving." But then, that 3 months turned into 9 and we kind of let it slide. We've picked up stuff as we've gone along. I called it restaurant Spanish. I'm pretty comfortable with all that kind of stuff, but conversation, no way. These countries allow us to be lazy, though.

Chelse is a friend of Gemma and Jason and a regular attendee at the women's retreat. She concurs that she has also been attempting to learn a few words in Spanish but has little faith that it will amount to much. She says:

> Well, I'm learning Spanish, but I will probably be learning Spanish for the rest of my life. Each time I go to a Spanish-speaking place, I'm realizing that I'm expanding my vocabulary a little bit. I'm like, "I didn't know what that sentence was 3 weeks ago and now I'm using it all the time!" And stuff like that.

Gemma, with support from her partner Jason, run the digital nomad women's retreat, so they are leaders in the subculture and introduce dozens of people to the lifestyle each year. But they find themselves in locations where they can get away with not learning the local language, because of the power of English-language domination, and their adherence to the tourist track. They choose not to go to locations where people may not speak English very much at all. While they discuss how the Thai language is radically different "for our western tongue," they admit that they also do not learn more than a few words in Spanish, even though they have spent significant amounts of time in Spanish-speaking countries. Chelse demonstrates that this is simply widespread for most digital nomads and tourists. Nate and Kam, the co-organizers of the conference, are also leaders in the field, but they do little to learn any other language and simply rely on English-dominance. Nate describes:

> I mentioned that Kam and I usually travel one month, or six weeks, in a place. That's enough time to get basic communication down. Words like, "Hello. Goodbye. How are you? The bill? Where is the toilet?" Maybe a little further than that. But, it's not really enough time to get fluent. Although I may be natural at programming languages, learning different verbal languages does not come naturally to me. Last year, Kam and I spent a month in Seoul, Korea. I already have forgotten all the Korean that I knew. I spent most of last year in Thailand. I remember almost no Thai, except for "Thank you." I have "Thank you" in Romanian, Portuguese, Spanish, etc. The only language I can really speak a little bit is Spanish, but I have very bad Spanish because I have used it so infrequently over the years. I can understand pretty well, and I can read incredibly well. But, then it's like, "Hello. A coffee please." Instead of "Hello, good sir. How are you today? It's beautiful weather out." I have really dumb sounding Spanish. I am hoping to improve that a little bit since our conference will be in Columbia next year.

There were very few participants who did learn a second language. Several already spoke multiple languages based on their heritage, but all of them had to learn English to be a world traveler and be a member of this community. Marcella is a 22-year-old American college student, who specifically studies linguistics and creative writing. She was inspired to travel from her love of language learning. She states:

> I am studying linguistics in college, it is a lot of theory, so I am still in theory mode. I would say my French is upper-intermediate, and I speak passable German, and Italian. I learned a little bit of Croatian, a little bit of Romanian. I lived in Georgia. I really try to learn a little bit when I go to the country. For example, in my thesis, I created a workbook for language learning that was immersive. I critique the Duolingo method; saying, "This is not how you learn a language, unfortunately. It is really easy but that is the problem." We like it because we can just pull out our phone and do 5 minutes a day but, in the end, it's wasted. I am super passionate about language learning. I am definitely going to continue to develop this workbook. However, I have been in theory mode for a while. A lot of people hear "linguistics" and say, "Oh, what languages do you speak?" and "Most linguistic docs speak a second language." It's the study of language. I studied language education. It is definitely not about the study of secondary language. It's about how language works.

Taylor is the only participant who learned a second language successfully and has immersed herself among locals in her chosen location. She first learned Spanish while working as a camp counselor in Guatemala where only the camp director spoke English. She reports that she was basically able to learn the language after three weeks of immersion (the same amount of time Chelse reports learning a few sentences of Spanish). Taylor describes her language learning process:

> The camp in Guatemala is mostly adults. Some teenagers, but mostly adults. Yeah, they basically taught me Spanish. It was a crash course. My first 10 days there I learned so much Spanish. I was then so motivated to keep learning. It was actually rather easy after that. Well, I had no choice. The only person who spoke English that was there was the director. We had become quite good friends. She is the one who originally worked in the camp in the United States. She was like, "Sorry. I'm just going to force you. Pretend that you can't ask me questions in English. It's just better." And, I didn't know anyone there, so there was no risk of embarrassment when I tried to say something. I just tried really hard to say it right. I think it was the best environment ever to learn at a rapid pace. Yeah, it was pretty easy after that. I went down again 6 months later just to be sure that I wanted to move there. I did some rouge volunteering. It was really fun. Just hopping place to place asking if they knew anyone else who needed help.

Taylor became passionate about this particular location – Guatemala – and her interest was particular to that country. She likes the country, the small touristy town of Antigua which still blended locals with expats. She admits that most of her friends are still expats, but she can easily socialize among the locals and chooses to do so. Taylor describes her life in Guatemala:

> I'm one of those people who is all about living like a local; even though, yes, most of my friends there are ex-pats and international. In Antigua and Guatemala specifically, the two populations that make up the city are ex-pats and native Guatemalans. They interact more than any place I have ever been. It's the best meshing. I can't explain it. I don't know why. The culture there is so heavy and so concentrated in such a small place that you kind of take on a bit of it. They are very welcoming, as well. There's something really unique about that place. I really love having Guatemalan friends.

Taylor says that she is a very slow traveler, mostly settling down in Guatemala, with a few, small excursions to nearby locations. This is one way to really learn about one place and one particular people. She is interested in learning more languages through this immersion technique. She describes her next goal:

> My next thing is definitely going to be Portuguese. I will definitely go to Portugal and live there. It's the Schengen zone, so I'll have 3 months. I would definitely love to go there by myself and learn Portuguese.

English speakers are accommodated most places in the globe – illuminating this postcolonial context where local people are forced to learn the global power language – but those native English speakers have little motivation to learn another language. Most travelers ignore this power dynamic inherent in English speaking. Additionally, it demonstrates a position of power when such travelers do not attempt to learn even a little of the language to speak to local people in their native tongue. Especially when they excuse themselves by saying it's difficult, rather than their lack of interest. After all, if something was difficult in relation to their business, they would be the first to say something using PP about the importance of embracing challenge. Thus, this behavior is enacting an unacknowledged power dynamic. Marcella is a passionate college student studying linguistics, but she also critiques the mainstream language learning platforms as being ineffective. Americans and British, in particular, are very resistant to learning other languages, while other Europeans of different linguistic backgrounds are broader in their abilities. Immersion, connecting to locals in meaningful ways, and staying in one place with an interest in the community are the proven ways in which people learn a second language.

Conclusion

This chapter begins with a look at the earliest family experiences of travel and how that impacts the participants. Some of the participants had immigrant and diasporic family backgrounds, which naturalized them to the processes of global living, but those were few. The majority of participants had quite standard family holidays of going to beach resorts, taking road trips to visit family members, and visiting Disneyworld. Some participants had parents who did not like to travel at all. The participants began traveling on their own after graduating from college. Some traveled before they discovered the digital nomad life, but others discovered the lifestyle on social media, which became their impetus for travel. Once participants did discover the digital nomad lifestyle, they quickly made the pilgrimage to Chiang Mai, Thailand, which has become ground zero for this lifestyle. They are attracted to the affordability, warm weather, and accommodating features of this tourist town. They mostly spend their time in coworking spaces, where they can meet other nomads like themselves, expats and Westerners, and can learn about business opportunities and networking events in such spaces. While the participants did not learn anything of the Thai language and blamed this on the language being too far removed from their own linguistic background, they equally did not learn the Spanish language, even when spending a great deal of time in Spain. Thus, while they had various theories on why they did not learn the languages of their locations visited, it simply comes down to them not being compelled to and a lack of interest. When Taylor found herself in an immersive experience without other English speakers, she ended up learning Spanish. None of the participants describe finding themselves in an immersive experience where they were not able to communicate in English. Thus, it seems that digital nomads are not overly interested in language learning, learning the cultures and politics of the locations they visit, nor shopping in local markets and learning to cook local food. Their visits remain on a superficial level where they seek out Western-style accommodations for living, coworking, and restaurant eating. This is surprising for a subculture that tries to distance itself from common tourists, who engage in similar superficial travels. Digital nomads pride themselves on having a travel lifestyle and staying in location for much longer than a usual holiday vacation. However, such in-depth time in countries does not connect them to the location on a deeper, more human-connection level.

Chapter 6

Seeking Same: Digital Nomads Seek Community

Introduction

Previous chapters have demonstrated that digital nomads place a great deal of effort and emphasis on leaving their homelands in order to travel globally, especially congregating in Southeast Asia, where they can leverage their unstable financial resources for access to a tropical, tourist destination. They protest the 8 hour workday and emphasize employment that centers most Westerners' lives. However, once they are embedded in the digital nomad lifestyle, they often feel isolated and lonely. Thus, they set out to find others like themselves – online or in person. This chapter provides an overview of the digital nomads' quest for community. After they leave their increasingly expensive and gentrified hometown, which they cannot afford, they discover digital nomadism, an alternative route to travel. But once overseas, they find themselves unable to speak the local language or engage with the locals on a meaningful level. They are strangers, perhaps for the first times in their lives. Therefore, they seek out community and relationships – with others like themselves – expats, backpackers, travelers, and digital nomads. This chapter talks about destination locations: from leaving their hometown to selecting a travel destination, participants also discuss issues related to traveling while female, finding co-living and coworking spaces, and their attempts at creating connections and community, both virtually and in real life.

Leaving Home: Neoliberal Financialization of Real Estate

> These leisure cities could accommodate, very affordably, the unemployed of the developed world and give them a more enjoyable lifestyle than many of them currently enjoy. (Makimoto & Manners, 1997, loc. 140)

In Makimoto and Manners (1997) manifesto, they foresaw that if workers were able to work remotely, they would likely choose to live somewhere vastly more

Digital Nomads Living on the Margins:
Remote-Working Laptop Entrepreneurs in the Gig Economy, 81–90

Published under exclusive licence by Emerald Publishing Limited
doi:10.1108/978-1-80071-545-520211007

affordable than their home nation could provide. Historically, in the United States, property was handed to, or financed by the state, for white residents: from The Homestead Act signed by President Lincoln in 1892, to President Roosevelt's Homeowners' Loan Corporation, to the creation of the Federal Housing Administration (FHA), and the Veterans Administration loan program. In contrast, black Americans faced formal segregation initiated by the state, and reinforced by the banks, through such processes as racial zoning, public housing regulation, subsidies for whites-only suburbs, tax exemptions for discriminatory institutions, redlining, and extrajudicial assault on black property (Blackwell & McAfee, 2020; Rothstein, 2018). More recently, predatory loans were approved, especially for people of color, who paid higher interest rates, and faced very high default rates during the 2008 recession, pushing many out of their homes. In 2008, nearly 80% of the nation's houses declined in value in 100 top market cities, the steepest decline in a generation (Wasik, 2009, p. 3).

The current phase of home ownership is one of "financification" (Hackworth, 2006). Globally, real estate is worth $217 trillion, comprising 60% of the world's assets (S. Stein, 2019, p. 2). In 2016, in the United States, a record 37% of homes bought were by absentee investors (S. Stein, 2019, p. 3). The real estate industry wields enormous power financially and politically – "between 2000 and 2016, real estate interests gave over $83 million to the state politicians who control New York City's rent and tax laws" (S. Stein, 2019, p. 80). Real estate shapes itself to the contemporary social trajectory, and for now, it is one tool of investment capital (D. Harvey, 1985, p. 83).

The pushing out of low-income long-term residents to locations further outside of the city so that properties can be marketed to high-income residents is the process of gentrification that is transpiring globally – the symbolic knife-edge of neoliberal urbanism (Hackworth, 2006; Zukin, 2014). The supply of affordable housing is decreasing rapidly, and there is not a single county in the United States where a full-time minimum-wage worker can afford a two-bedroom apartment (S. Stein, 2019, p. 3). In 2002, 50% of Americans could afford a modest house, which was at the beginning of the housing bubble (Wasik, 2009, p. 5). By 2005, half of the mortgages had buyers putting down nothing at all, while the median down payment was 2% (Wasik, 2009, p. 5). Mid-sized cities – Seattle, Portland, and Denver – were now the fastest growing (S. Stein, 2019, p. 3).

Community Envisioned

Community refers to a group of people unified through a location, characteristic, common interest, a shared professional interested, and so on. It refers to a group of people who identify with one another over a unifying concept, and location is significant in bringing the community together physically. Bauman (2012) calls it an old fashion togetherness, sameness, or:

> "Community" is these days the last relic of the old-time utopias of the good society; it stands for whatever has been left of the dreams of a better life shared with better neighbors all following better rules of cohabitation. (p. 92)

De Tocqueville (2002) wrote his two-volume *Democracy in America* after traveling through the young America, in the 1830s, and he was struck by the practice of democracy and the vibrancy of civil society – it was a country in which people joined associations of all stripes in order to come together with their fellow citizens to discuss current event and ideas. Forming such associations and civic participation remains in some ways, though Ikegami (2000) demonstrates how individuals might be a member of different types of non-overlapping networks, becoming fragmented. Bauman (2012) discusses the concept of "carnival communities," celebratory moments of alternative possibilities that offer a "temporary respite" from the usual social norms, and this break from the expectation, which opens up an ability to envision an alternative society, if only temporarily. Anarchist theory focuses heavily on the concept of constructed communities – "collectivism, anarchist communism, and anarcho-syndicalism" along with the central concept of mutual aid (Woodcock, 1962, p. 20). Anarchists believe in people's ability to live freely and collectively in order to work together with others to construct a society based on mutual aid and support (Vaneigem, 2001, p. 247; Woodcock, 1962, p. 22). Bookchin (1971) says a shift away from normative lifestyle structures can be a step toward utopia: "In the very act of refusing to live by bourgeois strictures, the first seeds of the utopian lifestyles are planted" (p. 16). The digital nomads are looking to abandon the expected path of full-time employment, hyper-consumerism, childrearing, and home ownership in expensive Western cities. Instead, they want to explore the possibilities of having experiences. They invert work and leisure. They select their destination based on leisure-desires and pleasure.

Women, Travel Destinations, and Networks

Gender influences destination selection. Is one traveling alone or with a male partner? By selecting a location for leisure and luxury, one must also be comfortable and relatively shielded from street harassment. Such images of danger are what friends and family back home caution about, often overlooking the relatively dangerous state of existence in the United States. Women are used to being cautioned about traveling alone in the world, or for being especially adventurous (E. Green & Singelton, 2006; Mzezewa & Moore, 2019; Specia & Mzezewa, 2019). Women are constantly cautioned to avoid "danger," solo travel, hedonistic leisure practices, and other freedoms that white men can engage in without question (Kugel, 2011). However, the risks of gender-based violence that women face is often already in their homes, their workplaces, and lurks in all corners of society. Women can certainly face increased rates of street harassment in various countries and cities, but such behaviors are easy to encounter in the streets of New York City as well. Women are trained to be cautious from a young age; they are living in a world in which their gender is often targeted for violence. Race, ethnicity, nationality all come together to position one's self in context. After resisting this fear mongering and becoming a woman traveling alone, perhaps anxious to unite with other digital nomads, the male-dominated spaces and sexism in such communities can be further disheartening. These networking spaces are important – especially for digital nomad development. Our networks are based on our previously established interests, professional connections, friends, acquaintances, and online communities (Barabasi, 2009). In network theories, "weak ties" or acquaintances provide the best bridges to the outside world, since our good friends are often very similar to ourselves, whereas acquaintances can be different enough to provide different knowledge, insight, connections, and resources (Barabasi, 2009, p. 43).

Co-living Spaces and Coworking Spaces

Young adults in their hometowns may live with roommates and friends for years after high school, or college, as they attempt to earn enough to support their own lifestyle. Their traveling may be similar: co-living with other young adults in hostels, or shared homes via Airbnb, can provide one with instant contacts, potential company, and friendship. Such shared spaces and co-living arrangements are now springing up in major metropolitan cities globally, as an alternative living situation, where the rents are sky high (Jiao & Wegmann, 2018). Thus, the model of co-living has gone from one for travelers, to include domestic living in one's own country, providing a more affordable and communal option. The majority of participants in this study live primarily, and almost exclusively, in Airbnb short-term rentals during their global travels, providing income to local residents who rent their personal properties out to travelers (Schor, 2017). Airbnb slashed 25% of its workforce in the aftermath of the COVID-19 pandemic, firing 1,900 workers (Sharma, 2020). However, months later, after losing half of the company's value in one year, from $35 billion to $18 billion, the company announced plans to go public by filing an initial public offering (IPO) (Driebusch, Farrell, & Lombardo, 2020). While digital nomads are often micro-entrepreneurs themselves, with some having previous experience working as a software engineer or with a start-up tech company, this demonstrates that the digital nomad lifestyle is heavily reliant on small, tech companies, demonstrating the unstable foundation upon which the lifestyle rests.

Coworking spaces are offices that provide short-term space to workers in need of office resources as well as social activities and a sense of community (Putra & Agirachman, 2016, p. 169). This business model originated post-2008 recession, exploiting the opportunity of accessing property after the significant losses in real estate (Gandini, 2015, p. 195). Most spectacularly, the story of the WeWork company, with major investments from SoftBank in particular, reach a peak of a $47 billion valuation, dominating the industry globally, before it's incredible crash (Bloomberg, 2019). The COVID-19 pandemic has closed many of the offices and led to a devastating drop in the space-sharing model of business. The topic of coworking has been a popular one, from business magazines to scholarly research. Makimoto and Manners (1997) foresaw the need for a coworking space as well:

> If employees are in the office for only a quarter of their working time, it makes sense to have four people to a desk ... thus instead of having personalized workspaces, every workspace has to be

> usable by everyone and every space will have a networked computer which anyone can use. (loc. 482)

Micro-entrepreneurs have especially been attracted to such facilities, especially the promoted idea of creating a community and cross-fertilization with other micro-entrepreneurs to foster business growth. As we learned from the rise and fall of WeWork, which was propped up artificially by SoftBank, the community outcomes are more mixed, especially for those who are not white men in the technology industry. Yeji Julia Cheon, a Korean nomad who travels and co-works in Southeast Asia, notes that among the mostly Western workers in the spaces, she feels invisible and excluded. Because of this, she works on creating her own business which connected Asian digital nomads to each other and the larger community, fostering a support system (Putra & Agirachman, 2016, p. 175). Müller (2016) notes the rise of such spaces but questions their widespread adaptation and how nomads and other entrepreneurs actually use such spaces. The nomads in this study – outside of Chiang Mai, Thailand, where coworking spaces were social spaces for nomads – did not prefer to work in coworking spaces and only two preferred such places. For Mariza, she enjoys such places because of her quest for socializing:

> I tend to like working in co-working spaces and cafes because I'm an extrovert. When I first got to Bulgaria, I was like, "Okay. I've got to finish this guide." I was punishing myself. "I'm not allowed to leave the house until I finish it." And it took longer because when I'm alone, I get tired. Like, "Maybe I should do some laundry. Maybe I should cook something." I get very distracted. For me, in order to focus more, I have to be around people.

Mariza enjoys working around other people, so she sought out coworking spaces in which she could socialize and meet people. For Marie, a computer programmer, she enjoys the space for work in conjunction with working out of the house.

> I would say 50% co-working spaces and 50% home. At the beginning, I made the mistake of only staying at home. The problem is, if you don't go out at night and meet people, after 3 days, you get cabin fever and you're willing to go anywhere just to talk to a human being. In those 3 months, I learned a lot about the digital nomad lifestyle. One other thing I discovered about myself is that I need to spend at least 50% of my time in a co-working space just to be around other people, talk to them, and not be by myself.

Both Mariza and Marie were interested in the social elements of coworking spaces, as they did not mention the access to resources such as printers and meeting space with clients, nor the formal events such as lectures and networking meetings that such spaces host. They enjoyed working while with other people, with the ability to connect with others, although this may happen less than they would like. Rather than office equipment, these nomads are signifying their desire to work in a social or public space.

Nomad Organizations: From Online to in Person Meetups

For the majority of nomads interviewed, they discovered the lifestyle on social media before they attempted to adopt it for themselves. A minority of others were already traveling and living nomadically, when they discovered that their own lifestyle had a label, identity, and subculture already attached to it. Nearly all of the nomads did seek out a sense of community within this shared lifestyle. Hannonen (2020) explores how some digital nomad travel bloggers stage authenticity for an audience by creating imagery that highlight technology and fast mobilities, while at the same time presenting themselves as quasi-professional travel bloggers rather than simply a hobbyist, in order to develop a community around this identity. And as the subculture was a male-dominated one, as some called the stereotypical participants "bro-mads," women especially, sought out spaces that were more inclusive. Marie is a white woman, computer programmer, who holds both Canadian and French passports. She is involved in organizations that promote women working in software, computer programming, and technology, often wearing T-shirts that signify these organizations. Marie states:

> What I can tell you, however, is that I am in this online group called Nomad Lists on Slack. You probably haven't heard of it, but it is like a chat group. This group has thousands of digital nomads, and a lot of them are dudes. The conversation is usually dominated by men. There is a section that is female only and so it has been really nice to be in this section in particular, it's only for women digital nomads. It has been interesting. Definitely, different types of conversations.

By having prominent digital nomad groups dominated by white men, especially in a group with thousands of members, it can create a hostile and chilling effect on women, people of color, LGBT folks, and other marginalized communities. Jay is also a web designer and tech worker, assisting clients remotely on their tech needs. While growing up in a fundamentalist conservative religious household and studying at a religious college in the United States, she is also a lesbian traveler seeking community in these various communities. She finds most of her social outlets on Facebook and Meetup.com, from which she does meet people in real life. Jay states:

> I'm part of a few digital nomad groups on Facebook. 7in7 was my first in-person experience with other nomads, which was really awesome. I didn't realize until I was there how lonely I'd been during the last 2 years, being out on my own. I tend to just reach out amongst my networks and say, "Hey, I'm looking at being in this

> area. Does anyone know people I should connect with while I'm there?" The problem is that all of them are location-based. They live in that space. So, I show up as this enigma and people aren't sure how to connect with me because they're like, "You're going to leave in 2 months. I don't want to get to know you too well." You know, like, "I don't want to get too attached to you!" There is some level of disconnect in the relatability because they are like, "I love what you're doing. I wish I could do that." But then, it's like they want to talk about their regular job and problems they have with their landlord. These location-specific topics. I'm like, "Yeah, that sucks. I don't know what to tell you." You know? I run my own business and don't have a landlord. So, it's very different.

The nomads rely heavily on social media and online groups to discuss their lifestyle issues and to find other travelers with whom they can meet up. Liza was originally from a family that had always been nomadic and diasporic. Liza states:

> I would say I haven't connected with the digital nomad community. I know location-independent people, but very few of them are in a community. One of my clients introduced me to this community. This is the first time I have spent any time with other location-independent people. Occasionally, I have conversations with clients about the lifestyle: "Isn't it weird to be at someone's house and they have big things? Like big shampoo. Bloody big things. Books!" It was at this conference that I met a large group of people, because I don't go to co-working spaces. I don't meet the sort of person who goes to co-working spaces. For me, nomads go to co-working spaces. When I'm in New York, say, I don't know how well you know Williamsburg, it's full of people working in coffee shops. Well, I can't do that because the internet is not good enough, I'm going to annoy all the people around me, and there is no client confidentiality. I go there for coffee and then go home to my place. So, the community I make is the community of other people doing my sort of jobs as opposed to nomads.

Even within the shared lifestyle – it is not enough to ensure that a community develops – and many people continue to be isolated in their remote lifestyles. Liza mentions that she is not interested in coworking spaces, which echoes other participants. Coworking spaces can be expensive and offer little for the price, besides desk space and a few drinks. Most prefer the comforts of their Airbnb temporary homes for work.

Digital nomads can be isolated and seek out others in the lifestyle, as their friends and family back home often do not understand it. To fill this need, many conferences promoting the digital nomad lifestyle, in addition to smaller retreats, or long-term co-living programs has arisen – a niche market in itself. For example, one can live in five megacities via the Roam.co corporate model, which provides a hotel-like bedroom and bathroom, with access to shared spaces. The company will even ship one's belongings to one of their other sites, in case a nomad wanted to simply rotate among top cities. The company, Remote Year, brings together a cohort of several dozen people for four months, up to a year, during which they rotate between cities each month, and move as a group, with the company managing logistics. Their business model suffered under the COVID-19 pandemic in 2020 and laid off the majority of its staff and left travelers stranded without refund as their business tumbled (Anand, 2020). Many of these small businesses that cater to travelers will disappear in response to the pandemic shutdown. Another business unlikely to survive the pandemic closures is that of Nomad Cruise, founded by Johannes Voelkner, a company that organizes two-week-long networking cruses for digital nomads twice a year that attracts around 150 international people per trip (Mohen, 2017).

The conference specifically set out to be a space where 75% of their invited speakers would be women, people of color, and LGBT community folks, a recruitment process that is advertised on their website, thus setting out specifically to be a space for minorities in the larger subculture. Co-organizer Kelly, herself a LGBT-identified nomad, states:

> I definitely participate in a bunch of communities online. Then, I created a community, as opposed to going to other events. We have been hosting our conference for about 2-and-a-half years. It has been my main community. It is very much my life. I generally meet a whole bunch of people from around the world there throughout the year. I do join the nomad communities in the cities that we're in. So, when we go to Budapest, there's a meetup tonight for digital nomads that I think we might head to. I guess I don't seek them out as much as I should. Mostly, I meet my nomads and connections online through social media. If they happen to be in the same city, we'll meet up and hang out.

As Kelly states, this was a way for these three friends to bring their community of approximately 75 people together for an extended event, where they, or their guests, could educate each other on the most current topics within the subculture. This provided them a forum to invite speakers that they admired within the community. The other co-organizer, Kam, agrees that she easily networks with her digital nomad friend and acquaintances on the web, she states:

> Once you meet one nomad, it's like, "Oh, let me introduce you to my friends." Then, they introduce you to their friends, who introduce you to their friends. That is the kind of way anybody makes community anywhere. That's pretty much how I formed my network of nomad friends. I think that is what really made nomad life sustainable for me. It can't be a solo endeavor forever. It's not possible. Just a few days ago, I was in London with one of our friends. She brought along another friend who is a nomad. He

> was saying how he really wanted to just focus on connecting with locals where he went; and he wasn't interested in connecting with other nomads. He also complained about how his friends in London were worried about him and didn't get what he was doing. They thought that he was crazy. I was like, "Listen. Absolutely. You need to connect with local communities, that's great. But, unless you're moving to that community permanently, if you're going to keep the nomad thing going, you need people who get that. Otherwise, you're alone. If your friends back home think you're crazy and the locals probably think you're crazy ..."

Thus, Kam places equal significance on nomads connecting with other nomads, as well as local connections. Yet, in the digital nomad subculture, they often favored meeting other nomads over local residents. Kaylee was an invited speaker to the conference, an older African American who was nearing retirement and had a full career working with a utility company in the United States. She was the only nomad to have (grown) children. Kaylee's traveling adventure was just beginning:

> I met people who actually talk like me. Before the conference, when I would say, "We're going to Europe. We're gone for three months. We're going to Spain, Greece, then Italy." It sounds wild. When people would ask me, "Where's your home base?" Well, kind of San Diego, but I really don't have one. Then, when I got to the conference, everyone was saying the same thing! People are naming off all these places! Even places I hadn't even heard of. I was like, "Oh, my God! These are my peeps!" Now I don't feel weird saying it because there are at least 78 other people around here saying the same thing I do. It brought the concept home for me.

Kaylee was one of the speakers on the mainstage of the conference, and her experience at the event was a welcoming one, at which she easily met and engaged with other women of color who were traveling. Some of whom she hoped to meet up with again during further adventures or at least reconnect with at the same conference the following year. Anna was a volunteer at the conference, having previously be-friended the group of friends at another event and thus enjoying the reunion:

> I am somewhat active in some of the digital nomad groups. But I like having a smaller group of close friends. I had a bunch of friends that I was really close during the first year that I was traveling, but then, a lot of them have stopped traveling. That's a reason why I attended the conference, because I needed to make new friends on the road. I stay in touch with them. I travel to places where I have friends. I have certain requirements that I need. I need decent internet, vaguely vegetarian friendly, and good weather. I'm not

> going to go on a ski-cation ever. Coming to Columbia was kind of determined because my friends are going to be here in January. I wanted to go to Argentina because I have some friends there, not nomads. I'm going to Machu Picchu in early January and the flights were just really, really expensive for Buenos Aires.

The conference was intentional in their aim to be a space for minority community members to gather, make friends, and discuss issues important to them, for example, connecting a social justice orientation to the lifestyle. A feminist and anti-racist approach to traveling is what they wanted to offer. Speakers were invited and thus provided a manicured, diverse group of attendees to speak on a wide range of topics. The conference had interaction guidelines that prohibited discriminatory practices, speech, or harassment. These were things overlooked at the mainstream nomadic events.

Conclusion

The participants all expressed their need for a specific nomadic community which could understand their chosen lifestyle and offer mentoring and advice on how to continue their nomadic adventure. This community also enjoyed gathering together for two weeks in a co-living house after each annual event to reconnect on a long-term basis. Some of them chose to travel together for months at a time, before branching off onto their own travel trajectories. This was especially helpful for the single women travelers who could reduce the harassment they received in certain locations if they were together with other people. It also assisted their ability to afford nicer, shared places. A subset of the conference attendees did enjoy spending weeks together and formed a tight-knit group at the center of the event. For many of them, they only attended one or two events each year, but all of them were very active in group forums online. Overall, their lifestyle was one of isolation and loneliness by definition, and such conferences and retreats offered a social lifeline to their otherwise solitary existence.

Chapter 7

Marginalized Identities, Social Justice, and Volun-tourism

Introduction

All aspects of the tourism industry are predicated on an assumed white and middle-class traveler from a Western nation. From the desired locations, the motivation, or the models represented in the advertisement image – we can see this stereotypical embodiment come to life. This chapter overviews how marginalized communities may have different desires, and social issues, when traveling aboard. This ongoing marginalization impacts the digital nomad community especially, as it is an even more selected and niche subsection of the tourism population. If we examine travelers of color, solo women travelers, the LGBT community, and people with disabilities, they may have other destination locations, motivations, and interests. For example, heritage travel interests can lead tourists to different destinations around the globe, rather than the overburdened main attractions. Dillette (2020) conducts an ethnography of African American travelers to Ghana for the symbolic year of 2019, "The Year of Return," a tourism campaign to commemorate the 400th anniversary of the first slave ship landing in America. This trip had a personal impact upon the travelers' own self-understanding, historical knowledge, and commitment to social justice. Dillette (2020) points out that it is rare that tourism is linked to social justice. We see this reflected in digital nomads' relative lack of interest in political connection or protest. But Dillette (2020) points to the ignited interest in social justice, and education, as a positive potential outcome of a root or heritage tour. Roundtree (2002) writes about the religious meanings of journeys made on "Goddess pilgrims," by women who belong to the Goddess movement. From their journeys to these sacred sites, they express and reaffirm their religious identity and political consciousness. Indigenous sites around the world are popular tourist destinations. Such sites attempt to balance the impacts of over-tourism, environmental impact, their own control over the sites, and distributive community benefits. Pride parades, Mardi Gras, and LGBT cruises are other alternative destinations overlooked in mainstream brochures. People with disabilities have to put great effort into finding

Digital Nomads Living on the Margins:
Remote-Working Laptop Entrepreneurs in the Gig Economy, 91–100

doi:10.1108/978-1-80071-545-520211008

information on accessibility for tourist sites they would like to visit. This chapter will center these marginalized communities within tourism to examine the specific concerns they have, how such tours could lead to developing social justice frameworks and questioning whether this is simply another niche marketing endeavor for the industry.

Gender, Sexuality, and Travel

When women speak to others about their plans to travel alone – they are often cautioned about danger. Such cautions are specifically gendered – as men do not receive the volume of concerned that women receive (Mzezewa & Moore, 2019). Indeed, women do need to be more cautious in general, as most countries are heavily misogynistic (Berlatsky, 2020). However, the majority of violence that women face is by an intimate partner in their own home – and in their home countries (O'Toole, Schiffman, & Sullivan, 2020). For Americans, they face far higher rates of national gun violence than the majority of (post-)industrialized global countries. For American women, they indeed may be safer while outside of their home country. By following general security basics, women can travel alone without incident (Mzezewa & Moore, 2019). However, such cautionary advice has a chilling effect on women's enthusiasm for travel, and they are further exhausted by defending their leisure objectives (Jacoby, 2001). However, by one survey, the majority of solo travelers are women, and sometimes by high margins (Industry Global News 24, 2020). Women also have increasing control of larger discretionary spending abilities and should be an important market for the travel industry (Nielsen, 2020b). Interviewee Sara is an Arab American who has traveled throughout Middle Eastern countries. Sara describes her experience:

> It is definitely a different experience than it is if you're a male traveler traveling solo. I think, oftentimes, my experiences vary depending on the country that I am in; and also, the people that I end up meeting. I think it has been good, generally speaking. I find that in certain countries people are very in awe, or confused, as to how I could be a solo female traveler, how I could travel by myself. Of course, I think being Muslim and Arab also offered me a different kind of perspective and experience. People are very … Many people have very strong constructions about what it is like to be 1: Muslim; 2: A woman; and 3: to them, a woman traveling solo is probably something that they don't see very often. I think I do spend a fair amount of time explaining my lifestyle and how it fits into my culture and religion.

She has also traveled throughout Latin America, where she is perceived to be Latina, and therefore, people speak to her in Spanish. As a single traveler, she is often approached by men and has to manage the situation accordingly. And of course, some of the solo traveling women may indeed be open to dating while traveling and have their own holiday romances (J. S. Taylor, 2001). One study discusses how women use the freedom of being away from one's home context to be more open in their romance and sexuality choices while on vacation than they otherwise would behave back home (Berdychevsky, Gibson, & Poria, 2015).

LGBT

LGBT folks often examine the homophobic climate of their travel destination before committing to a place. First of all, 72 countries still criminalize same-sex sexual relationships, whereas 124 states have no legal penalties against same-sex sexual activity (Carroll & Mendos, 2017; Heil, 2019). Within these categories are a range of levels of dangers for travelers to consider. South Africa and Fiji are popular because of their constitutional antidiscrimination provisions (Puar, 2002, p. 108). LGBT-oriented group tours, accommodations, clubs, cruises, landmarks, and neighborhoods have sprung up, and this niche of tourism has become big business (Puar, 2002). LGBT folks may travel to LGBT-oriented locations, or take specific tours, in which they feel supported and included, in ways that they may not even feel back home. Others are simply not perceived as LGBT during their travels; and this may reduce it as an issue for them. Others may feel invisible, or that their relationship is not recognized. For Haley, she has not experience discrimination while traveling; in fact, she mentions that she faces the most discrimination in her home country:

> I can't say I've personally felt harassed or anything anywhere but in London. I've had the most issues about being queer in London. I've never been called out on anything. I've never had a weird look. Nothing. I think that's also due to the places I choose to go. I do tend to go to places where I know they're at least somewhat LGBTQ friendly. I'm not closed off to going to places that aren't, but I just want to be somewhere I feel comfortable. I don't feel like it's had any huge impact on me, if I'm honest. No. I feel freer in a lot of the places I've gone to than I ever have at home, so that's good, I guess.

Haley makes an important point that discrimination is not something "over there," located in a different country or culture, but is often experienced – like violence against women – in one's hometown and in one's own country. As they are able to choose their own travel destination, for those who are interested in more LGBT friendly locations, they may choose places where they feel great support. However, they may choose some locations based on other interests, places in which they do face harassment or discrimination. In one study of an Israeli lesbian's travel diary, she describes how the tourist accommodations provided the most sense of ease, compared to other locations such as the urban environment or her own home (Poria, 2006). Finally, if LGBT folks are interested in dating while traveling, they have to find the locations or online dating apps that provide the best options for their demographic. American participant Jay, who was raised in a fundamental religious household and later came out as a lesbian, states:

> I haven't figured out how to really effectively date in the nomad world yet. I think part of it is just the critical mass of nomads, particularly queer women nomads. It is just harder to connect with them. I have continued to use sites like OKCupid when I'm in a location. I've had a few experiences, aside from the girlfriend in Australia … When I was in southern California at the beginning of this year, I would get people who are like, "I'm up for a fling." And, I'm like, "No. I actually want a relationship." Or, I would get people who are like, "I want a relationship. Maybe I can convince you that you don't want to be a nomad anymore." So, neither of those are really great options. I have been continuously improving my profile on the sites: "I'm a nomad. I don't plan to stop being a nomad. I move every 2–3 months. Ideally, I am looking for somebody who wants to do that with me." And, I'm open to the idea of having a home base, but, you know, that would be something that would be discussed with said partner when I find her. I definitely haven't mastered that, yet! It's a work in progress.

Not only is it more of a challenge to find a LGBT partner because of the non-dominant status, but as nomads, they are interested in dating people who are most likely location-based, unless they date other nomads within the subculture. Many of the nomads who did not have partners found it very difficult to date while in the lifestyle. This was often a reason for one to settle down. Years after our interview, Jay found a partner in southern California and did get engaged. This stopped her traveling for the time being. Relationships are likely to be a big impetus for ending, or slowing down, their travels.

Race, Racism, and Travel

Nate's digital nomad conference collected demographic data on attendees and found that most were from Western nations with strong passports. He shares his guess on the demographics of travelers in general:

> They have money, privilege, and access to a high-quality passport. I would say, generally, when traveling the world, I mostly come across UK and Western European people. There are a lot of American nomads now, but a lot of American nomads stay in the United States. They are RV nomads, for example. You have Mexico, Canada, Central America, it's really easy to travel for years without necessarily flying across an ocean. If you hang out in Southeast Asia, you're going to get a lot of Aussies and Swedes, for some reason. Swedes are really well-traveled, apparently. I remember we captured demographic information for our conference and most people are from developed countries. I would say that if you took North America, Western Europe, the UK, Australia, and New Zealand, that's got to be at least two-thirds of everyone [in the digital nomad community].

Marketers in tourism often rely on an unspoken norm of whiteness, which we see reflected in advertisements and reviews of travel destinations (Urry & Larsen, 2011). However, for non-white travelers, they may give some consideration to the racial climate of a destination and the prevalence of overt racism. During transit alone, there are hundreds of reported incidents of abuse while flying:

> The International Air Transport Association reported that there were 350 reported cases of racial, homophobic, ageist, and sexual abuse on flights, and yet only one in 20 offenders were removed from planes. Police or security personnel were involved in only 178 of the incidents and 141 of the incidents resulted in a simple warning. The real kicker? Only 17 of the 350 passengers who engaged in discriminatory or abusive behavior were taken off the aircraft. (Temblador, 2018)

Indeed, in another report, 15% of African American travelers worried about racial profiling while traveling, 13% worried about airport harassment, and 11% worried about terrorism (Clausing, 2019).

By 2019, African American travelers had a reported $63 billion in spending, which makes them a large, and often overlooked market (Clausing, 2019). To fill this niche market, websites, companies, accommodations, and heritage tours have sprung up to address specific racial or ethnic groups and their leisure consumption. For example, Travel Noire (2020, https://travelnoire.com/), Black and Abroad (https://www.weareblackandabroad.com/), and Black Passport Stamps (https://blackpassportstamps.com/) are websites created for the black travel community, connecting them to black-owned hotels, businesses, and other leisure organizations. Another community was established by traveler Rondel Holder (2020), who set out to see the world but was surprised to see very few travel stories from the black perspective. He founded his website Soul Society 101, where he shares his own travel experiences as well as providing resources for other travelers. Other websites for black women have been developed to connect women to a community, including Black Adventuristas (https://www.blackadventuristas.com/) and Black Girls Travel, Too (https://www.blackgirlstraveltoo.com/).

The digital nomad literature is also lacking in racial diversity representation as Hopkins (2019) writes, including the voices of nomads of color who do seek out information oriented to their racial demographic:

> There's seemingly no representation of diversity in the location independent community. Considering the obstacles minorities have faced in the U.S., many weren't necessarily rushing to enter countries with potentially similar societal issues. With the absence of awareness, among other things, people simply didn't know what to expect, while some just weren't comfortable making those kinds of leaps. "Sometimes, people weren't necessarily supportive of it," said Fluker. "When I was younger, a lot of my friends weren't encouraged to travel outside the country

> because it wasn't something our parents did. My parents didn't know what was going on. There wasn't social media. It was just different."

Edokpayi (2020) also writes on the significance of black women nomads and what they contribute to the world of travel information and insight:

> Sencherey also shared her experiences as a Black woman abroad, describing a range of experiences in Brazil, Montenegro, South Africa and other countries where she faced blatantly racist acts. "One thing that I now know for sure is that the world doesn't really know who women of color are, especially those from the U.S. They have a stereotypical view of us from the media and Hollywood – I've often been referred to as Serena Williams, Beyonce, Obama Family. Our international identity is also mixed within the context of each country's own history with people of color and, more recently, those who have landed in their country for various reasons from Africa."

Black travelers have faced a fundamental lack of representation in travel material, promotional imagery, and information about travel and racism and have had to create their own material and community. The white establishment is only motivated for inclusion when they realize the significant amount of spending power travelers of color hold. For example, Nielsen (2020a) estimates that Asian Americans have a buying power of $1.2 trillion, whereas black and Latinx consumers also have significant consumer power. Travelers themselves build their own communities in the grassroots, by promoting and interviewing each other. For example, the blogger who goes by The Awkward Traveller (2019) wrote a website post promoting 40 Asian American travel bloggers in order to counteract such invisibility. This representation is significant for people of color. While white people see themselves everywhere – the lack of representation for people of color impacts their communities and also erases the significance of travelers of color in mainstream images. Participant Hannah shares how racism and stereotype cloud her experiences while traveling and her interactions with locals. Hannah states:

> I think a lot of times people expect me to say that I'm Chinese. But when they see my mannerisms then they're like, "You speak English really well." For me it doesn't bother me that much because I do realize that it's an inherent bias, a very cultural bias that if they see a Chinese person, they expect them to be Chinese, talk about Chinese things, and share more Chinese culture. That's another way to earn trust. Like for me it's like if I share the part of my culture more then they're more like, "Oh, interesting. This person is real, this person is believable, and I can understand this person." But if I shared the Canadian part that might throw them off. They might be like, "She's suspicious and she's foreign."

Organizing specific communities is significant for those who do not see themselves in the media, who may not see their community members traveling in the ways that white people do and want to connect with others like themselves. For example, the organization Latinas Who Travel is an online bilingual community that brings Latinas together for group tours, to promote women-owned businesses, and to provide bilingual access to tourist information (Nunez, 2018).

The Journal of Sustainable Tourism published a special issue on Sustainable Tourism and Indigenous Peoples, with 16 papers on a variety of topics. Indigenous tourism has often been developed to open one's culture and sites in order to gain economic benefit for the community (Carr, Ruhanen, & Whitford, 2016). Indigenous communities are often committed to sustainable practices, but high volumes of tourists compromise such efforts. Pereiro (2016) finds this balance is difficult to achieve in indigenous communities in Latin America, where more community members could empower themselves by expansion to digital media, and to increased involvement in local governance. The articles speak of global indigenous cultures and their host tourism practices, but the topic of indigenous travelers themselves is left unexplored.

Accessible Travel and Disability

In 1986, the United States passed the Air Carrier Access Act, which stated in part:

> A person with a disability may have a physical or mental impairment that impacts a major life activity – such as walking, hearing, or breathing. This may be on a permanent or temporary basis. For example, a person with a temporary disability may have a broken leg that is temporarily fused or immobilized. Airlines must accommodate the needs of air travelers with disabilities. (US Department of Transportation, 1986)

In 1990, President Bush signed the Americans with Disabilities Act (ADA) and made it illegal to discriminate against people with disabilities. However, enforcement is left to the US Department of Transportation, without a budget for such operations. Therefore, complaints are usually made against companies through human rights offices, and businesses are told to comply after a successful complaint is processed; however, it can take a great deal of time. Clear protocol of what is required to make a space accessible is often not expansive enough for many people with disabilities (Cerchiai & Lieberman, 2018). The US Census estimates the number of Americans with disabilities at 20% of the population or 56.7 million people (Cerchiai & Lieberman, 2018). The Open Doors Organization (2015), which fights for equal access for consumer practices, especially in travel and leisure, estimates that adults with disabilities spend $17.3 billion each year, and it could be a much greater figure if there were accessible options. Furthermore, representation of people with disabilities in travel materials is of significance not only for representation alone but to demonstrate accessibility and to include explicit, detailed information. Benjamin, Bottone, and Lee (2020) examine 200 county-level travel brochures in the Southeast United States to examine whether people with disabilities are represented. They also follow-up with interviews with state-level tourism marketing directors, in order to understand their approach to accessibility. The researchers found these managers' understanding of accessibility to be lacking. Chikuta, du Plessis, and Saayman (2017) found in their research that people with disabilities are very much interested in visiting national parks for the same motivating factors as non-disabled people. While Benjamin et al. (2020) found that most tourism managers felt that ADA compliant was good enough, the ADA is a minimum bar for accessibility, and extended efforts would reach more people. The Critical Design Lab (2020) is doing just that. This interdisciplinary laboratory is a participatory data collection and accessibility mapping project that is informed by disability justice, intersectionality, and a critical design perspective. Aimi Hamrale (2017), a member of the laboratory, published *Building Access: Universal Design and the Politics of Disability*, which investigates the twentieth-century strategies of design for disability. Accessibility regulations are developed after people pressure the government for such; thus, they are born out of social movement struggles and the disability rights movement has contributed a great deal to the final signing of such laws. But continued pressure is important for reporting non-compliant business, documenting accessibility with online reviews, and hosting events in accessible spaces. The pandemic has shifted many venues online, and this has created an opening for people with disabilities to attend events and spaces that they previously were not invited into (Beery, 2020).

While few and far between, there are a few tourism books specifically targeted to travelers with disabilities, providing important accessibility information and reviews (Ingram, 2018). There are anthologies sharing firsthand voices of people with disabilities speaking on all aspects of their lives (Catapano & Garland-Thomson, 2019; Lalvani, 2019; Wong, 2020). And there are travel bloggers who write on accessible travel locations and run active social media sites posting pictures of themselves, reviewing and enjoying many global locations. John Morris (2020) is an avid traveler who runs the website Wheelchair Travel – Accessible Travel Blog. Cory Lee (2020) is a travel enthusiast who uses a wheelchair, and he reviews locations for accessibility for his blog *Curb Free With Cory Lee*.

Volun-tourism as Alternative Travel

The tourism industry as a whole is structured in a way that multinational corporations dominate and collect huge revenue from their global branches, with very little money trickling down to the local economy (Lansing & de Vries, 2007). Airlines, hotel chains, corporate Airbnb rentals, cruise shifts, and all-inclusive resorts are some examples of these global industries. This makes local communities vulnerable to changes in the tourist market, but the multinationals are more insulated with their size and diversified companies. Volunteer tourism – or volun-tourism – is a niche market in tourism but not an insignificant one. In one estimate, more than 1.6 million young people (primarily white women) from the global North travel to the global south to volunteer and end up spending two billion annually (Bandyopadhyay & Vrushali, 2017). In Bo et al. (2020) survey of volunteer tourists, they found that motivation for becoming a volunteer were connected to enacting personal values and increased feelings of self-worth. This reinforces the findings of Bandyopadhyay and Vrushali (2017), who write on the use of volunteers taking selfie photos with the local community with which they work, often children of color, and such images are posted on social media to present a particular construction of the self (p. 8). Freidus (2017) presents a critique of the volunteer tourism trend by pointing out that such visits are short-term, offer few skilled volunteers, and that the volunteers should be educated on the structural inequalities and postcolonial histories that are an important aspect of understanding the current situation in such locations. Freidus (2017) encourages volunteers with skills to engage in long-term commitments to such volunteer opportunities. Only two of the interviewees had participated in volunteer tourism: one American who joined the Peace Corps for two years with her husband. And Taylor who had volunteer for a camp four years in a row and then took the opportunity to volunteer at a similar camp in Guatemala for 10 days in a work exchange for lodging. It changed her life and led to her long-term commitment to the country:

> It was so random. I definitely didn't have any desire to. I know that sounds weird. I feel like everyone who grows up is like, "I've always wanted to travel." It was not like that for me. I simply was volunteering at a camp I had volunteered at for 4 years in a row. It's a camp for people with disabilities. They said, "Oh, one of the counsellors from the '80s – one of the volunteers – started a similar camp in Guatemala. She's looking for volunteers from our camp because you already know how to take care of people with disabilities. It doesn't matter if you know Spanish. If you want to go and pay for the flights, it is a 10-day vacation in Guatemala with people with disabilities." I was like, "Sign me up. Sure." I went by myself and it just completely changed my life. I flew back on the plane. I was like, "I have to quit teaching. I have to do something to get back into Central America again." I was completely changed forever.

Taylor's long-term commitment and embeddedness in Guatemala is different than the usual short-term and superficial travels of digital nomads. Her commitment to learning Spanish and engaging with locals in her adopted community are distinctive.

Conclusion

This chapter looks at marginalized communities often overlooked by the tourism industry. In other chapters, we have seen that the digital nomad community is often represented as white and male, but other nomads are creating their own events to target marginalized communities. This chapter takes a broader look at several marginalized demographics and what particular travel interests and concerns they may have. This chapter talked about how women often face cautions when telling others about their solo-travel desires, which can have a dampening effect on women's adventures. However, when examining the larger context of violence against women, we see that the dangers women face are most acutely within their own homes, and, certainly, within their own home countries. By representing danger lurking in other countries, we discount the high rates of violence in the United States, especially. We then turn to look at travelers of color and how their marginalization has led to a mini industry, which specifically tries to appeal to travelers based on race, and perhaps offering roots or heritage tours to different places off the beaten path. Travelers with various mobility and sensory disabilities face a labyrinth of accessibility challenges. While in the United States, accessibility minimum standards are legislated (if not adequately enforced), other countries fair far worse and may not even have such requirements. Therefore, for travelers with disabilities, seeking out accessibility information before taking the trip is important. A few bloggers address these issues but extremely few. For all tourists to include accessibility information in their reviews of venues and destinations can be an act of solidarity and visibility. Finally, this chapter looks at volun-tourism, as an industry in itself, which attracts (overwhelmingly white) young women to the global south to engage in short-term volunteer projects, organized by colleges or non-profit organization. However, critics of these practices point to the dangers of such programs. The tourist industry should widen its audience to specific demographics, listen to their interests and desires, and create other tourist pathways that appeal to a wider swath of the population. However, as we will see in the next chapter, perhaps continued and broadening expansion of tourist consumption is not a positive development for environmental and social outcomes. While expanding business and target markets does not challenge the ravages of tourism and consumption, the next chapter applies a more radical critique about the impacts of travel on the environment and social inequalities.

Chapter 8

Digital Nomads as Canaries in the Coalmine: Disruption and the Future of Work and Leisure

Introduction

In *The Illusion of the End*, Baudrillard (1994) argues against the idea that the future is linear and progressive. History is constantly in the process of revision. The ideals of Keynesian economics continue to reverberate, even while the concepts of full employment and social safety nets are eroded. In this chapter, we begin to look toward the future of digital nomadism. As the chapter is being written, the COVID-19 pandemic still rages across the globe, causing overwhelming disruption – especially to the digital nomad lifestyle. This disruptive moment provides us the space to look in multiple directions to speculate on what the future might hold as we navigate and look to a post-pandemic future. The impact of the pandemic was divided for the digital nomad community. On the one hand, it expanded remote work to untold millions of white-collar office workers. Thus, the world became familiarized with the concept of remote work in an instant. While nomads were already accustomed to working from home, they may have seen their online businesses or revenue be negatively impact by declining sales. On the other hand – travel halted. Digital nomads were either stranded in a host location or were locked down in their own country. We will look at the future of digital nomadism in the context of the pandemic, as an example disruption, which we can expect more of in relation to environmental catastrophes, mass migration, and economic contractions. Considering this context of borders closed for health outbreaks, nomads may shift to domestic and slow travel, or may consider establishing a home base and pausing their nomadic aspect. In the larger picture, we can question what the environmental impacts of global travel are upon the future of the planet and if the digital nomad lifestyle can be a sustainable one.

Digital Nomads Living on the Margins:
Remote-Working Laptop Entrepreneurs in the Gig Economy, 101–117

Published under exclusive licence by Emerald Publishing Limited
doi:10.1108/978-1-80071-545-520211009

The COVID-19 Pandemic and Disruption to Traditional Work

The COVID-19 pandemic of 2020 quickly shuttered economies, schools, international borders, and travel. People were told to stay home in quarantine and countries had a variety of strictness, which would impact the continued spread of the virus. The pandemic brought to light the decades of underfunding of social infrastructure and how quickly all that is solid melts into air (Berman, 1981). The United States was especially hard hit, with the worst number of cases and death globally. Because of this, most countries closed their borders to Americans in particular, thus demonstrating how one nation's esteemed global standing can dramatically shift (Higgins, 2020). In 2019, only 7.3 American workers described themselves as digital nomads, and the rate of remote work was 8.2% of the workforce (Bick, Blandin, & Mertens, 2020; MBO Partners, 2020). By March 2020, white-collar workers who could work remotely were allowed to do so, instantly familiarizing the world with the concept of remote work. As work shifted online, productivity increased in many cases (Morgan, 2019). Top tech firms took it the furthest by offering employees the ability to work remotely for a year or more. However, tens of millions of workers were laid off as their companies closed, faced hardships, or reduced their expenses. While workers filed for unemployment in the United States, which was briefly bolstered by an additional weekly $600 boost on top of their allotted payment, gig workers did not qualify for unemployment as independent contractors (although a federal short-term fund was created for them) (Brynjolfsson et al., 2020; Dickson, 2020; Lane, 2020; Sarkar-Basu, 2019).

Digital nomads were especially hard hit in the wake of the pandemic. Such disruptions are likely to continue with similar and increasingly volatile effect into the future, so examining the pandemic as an example of such is appropriate. The pandemic fallout did not have to occur in the manner it did. We can see that different nations' approaches did have different outcomes. However, we have not reverse course on starving public institutions and safety nets, so more extreme human suffering can be expected in the future. Nomads were quick to post their experiences on their blogs and YouTube channels. The Wandering Ravens (2020), a heterosexual digital nomad couple, shares their background – which resonates with the general demographics of nomads. The couple is originally from Seattle, and they have been traveling for over three years. They did not have a home base to which they could retreat. They write web-based travel content for income, which has since disappeared. They had been on the verge of a house-sitting engagement when the pandemic hit, and their plans were canceled. Considering the expense of returning to the United States – taxes, health insurance, rent, transportation – they were not keen on the idea of returning, and yet quarantining for an unknown amount of time is also intimidating. Nomads often cross borders in order to renew their tourist visa; such mobilities were no longer possible during the pandemic (Griffith, 2020). The digital nomad YouTube channel Support Adventure (2020) posted a video on "The Future of Digital Nomads: Post Coronavirus Predictions 2020," in which Eric and Tal speak of the future of nomadism from their location in Chiang Mai, Thailand. In this video they predict that digital nomadism will lose its mystique as remote work becomes normalized. These newly created remote workers may soon begin to question why they live in their expensive hometowns and consider moving abroad. However, too many people in the same locations will cause negative outcomes, such as financial and cultural gentrification. Eric and Tal point out that "slo-mads" was a growing concept before the pandemic and is likely to increase afterward – the idea of traveling slowly, for example, spending three months in a location rather than two weeks. Nomadic Matt (2020) is more dire in his outlook of the post-pandemic future:

> I think this fall we're going to see many tour operators, hostels, independent hotels, magazines, creators, and other businesses in this space go under. A bloodbath is coming. (And this site is not immune. We're barely treading water. At our current spend, we'll be bankrupt by Feb 2021 if something doesn't change.) But, while the job loss will be terrible, travel was in need of serious reform. It had simply grown too big. We were in a Gold Rush. From VC-backed startups to hostels to influencers to tour companies, there was just too much of everything. Overtourism was a huge problem. Destinations just weren't built to handle so many people and the environmental impact from all this travel was staggering.

Nomadic Matt (2020) points to the unsuitability of contemporary mass travel and the environmental outcomes. However, as he points out, we are at a crisis point of over-tourism, and the answer may be to stay local, likely an unpopular answer. The figures agree with his diagnostic. According to the World Travel & Tourism Council, the 2020 pandemic accounted for the global tourist industry to shed 121 million jobs, with losses projected to be around $3.4 trillion (Glusac, 2020).

Dysfunctioning Just Fine (2020) is another YouTube blogger, Meredith a theater performer, who creates content on topics of digital nomadism, chronic illness, disability, and LGBT identity, posted a video, "Disabled Digital Nomad Ep. 4: What it's Like Being a Nomad During a Pandemic." As a performer, Meredith has quickly lost 75% of her income, and writing makes up her other revenue streams. She has survived on work stays where she exchanges labor for lodgings; however, the engagement she had pre-pandemic ended quickly at the outset, pushing Meredith to return to her hometown of Cleveland. She has settled into an apartment where she can work on her play and use her wheelchair to go to the grocery store two blocks away, bringing along a suitcase to hold her purchases. For travelers with disabilities, and travelers with such marginal incomes, retreating to one's hometown still causes hardships, especially the high prices and healthcare costs (in the United States).

For participant Jemma, who sent an updated post-pandemic follow-up on her experience as a nomad, she has been able to weather the pandemic easier, with a few home bases from which she rotates, between Edinburgh, Scotland; The Algarve, Portugal; and Berlin. Jemma states:

> The only difference is, now I don't feel guilty if I'm working too much to get out and enjoy myself. Workwise, it's been fine. I'm a freelance copywriter and, while some of the niches I work in like travel and fashion have slowed down, other areas like alcohol and (surprisingly) events promotion have ramped up. I've been very lucky, but there have been ups and downs in terms of income. Luckily, I'm spending less on travel, so it evens out. Although I've been spending more on groceries, as I'm trying to support local businesses rather than supermarkets.

As a nomad working as a freelance writer, Jemma has managed to maintain, and even increase, her workload. As office workers shifted to remote work, newspaper articles proliferated as they covered this transition. *The New York Times* pointed out that full-time workers were enjoying the schedule flexibility, and with it, they were engaging in more personal care or spending more time with family (C. C. Miller, 2020; Strzemien, Bennett, Ma, & Lyons, 2020). Nomads who relied on small incomes based on selling Facebook ads or writing travel content have been hit hard by loss of income. Kathleen, a British nomad, updated me on her journey during the pandemic. Previously, she had a full-time job with a major airline for which she made a six-figure salary and was able to work remotely for the company. However, she was downsized and has been living off savings for 10 months, seeking employment while living off savings:

> The pandemic has done me a favor. There are more jobs now that would have been office based in London, that are now open to me. I'm currently looking for clients and work. And so, it's enabling me to reach companies that would have shut me out previously. One problem with the pandemic has been the level of competitiveness, lots of people are looking for work. I'm sure any nomads that are stuck in Chiang Mai might find it hard to generate revenue and income. Just because the pandemic right now has made it an incredibly competitive marketplace. I know one guy in Bali, he's running out of money because his co-living space has been shut down by this pandemic. So, he's now looking for alternative means of income. I think it must be really stressful if you're involved in business in traditional nomad population. They won't survive on this type of work.

With millions laid off globally, the increased among of remote work job seekers will escalate exponentially, driving up competition for jobs engaged in by nomads. However, as Kathleen presents, more office work will open to the idea of remote work, when they would have previously not considered such an option. This may also lead to increased attention by the government on how to more specifically tax remote workers, especially considering the devastating decrease in public revenue.

Creating a Home Base

The pandemic closed international borders; therefore, digital nomads and other travelers had to make quick decisions about where to ride out the pandemic shutdown. Their previous plans may have been canceled and their accommodations may have become unreliable. Before the pandemic, the digital nomads were not necessarily opposed to having a home base. Mel describes her desire:

> For us, it's more about being location independent. It's about the freedom to choose, not necessarily about living out of a backpack constantly. I think we need a home base at some point. At least the ability to choose where that home base is for a few months, and then to move on again. I guess that's the definition of digital nomad. Having your own stuff around is pretty cool. Sometimes you just need that home stuff to feel grounded, before you take off. I think we're at that point. I think we'll be on the road again within the next 12–18 months in some capacity, whatever that looks like: another country or just being able to move around home more easily.

Digital nomad Haley agrees. After years of work exchange and digital nomad travel, she looks forward to also having a home base in the future. Haley states:

> Hopefully I'll travel forever to an extent, but I do want to have some sort of home base. I want somewhere to keep books, to keep shoes, to keep nice things. I really struggle with the whole minimalist thing. I can't do it. I've just recently started traveling with checked baggage. When I buy things I like, I want to keep it. I also want a home for that sense of community. I want to invite friends over for dinner or go to a movie. A home base where I'd live maybe six months a year and then travel the rest would be really awesome. I do want to have kids at one point, and they will be nomad children.

The digital nomads do desire having their own space, where they can keep and collect their own things, while having some time of the year when they can travel. As the lifestyle has been portrayed as one of constant travel, some wonder whether one can take on the label while traveling only part of the year – but there is no set definition or path to which one must adhere. Overall, the nomadic itinerary is flexible and subject to change. Being hired by a location-based company, finding a romantic partner, or having a child are all likely to halt a nomad's travel trajectory.

Since the pandemic, I touched based with the digital nomads to see how their journey had evolved three years after our interview, and how the pandemic was impacting their current life. British Kathleen has been attempting to settle down in Portugal, but it remains a struggle:

> Since Javea, Spain I have been travelling for 1 and a half years. I became exhausted. I was meeting new friends, staying with friends, and always saying goodbye to people. It was really fun, initially, but then it became kind of exhausting. And each time I said goodbye to a new set of travel friends, I felt a little bit heartbroken. It was quite lonely. But then I think about superficial, just for fun friendships, as almost like junk food. It gives you a short-term hit, but then afterwards you long for something a bit more substantial. So, I settled in Portugal. But I'm thinking about leaving. I realize it's not multicultural like England. Lisbon was very popular with digital nomads, so it was easy to meet people. But when I tied to live outside of Lisbon, it was very much a village mentality, where they hadn't seen somebody of Asian descent before. And even if I was Portuguese and spoke Portuguese, I think it would still be difficult to settle here because people stick together with their friends from childhood and they're not open to foreigners. I've been an expat in Tokyo, Singapore, Dubai, and it's very transient. You meet people that work there for a few years and then they move on. It's never easy actually, being outside your own country.

Kathleen describes the relationships she has built on the road with other travelers as akin to junk food. Kathleen has been dedicated to spending her time in co-living and coworking spaces during her travels specifically in order to meet people and establish relationships. Indeed, she and I met in Javea, Spain, during the women's retreat, where we lived together for a week. She had a significant full-time job, for which she was able to negotiate working remotely. She had already spent a great deal of time traveling for the company. But she did long for more permanent friendships, and she has been settling down in Portugal, applying for residency and living in various towns and cities throughout the country. However, it has not been easy to assimilate. Kathleen makes the distinction of creating a new home base in Portugal, compared against if she had remained in her home of London and continued to work remotely:

> I think working from home is a lot harder. Because you don't have that community. You don't have the adventure. You can get bored, lonely, depressed. I think it's different, actually, working from home. I wouldn't have considered working from home from England. It would have been way too depressing. And way too expensive as well. I mean, just commuting to WeWork, and having to pay rent, would have cost me $2,000. With no added value whatsoever. I figured I could use that $2,000 to travel the world and work from Chiang Mai, to be honest. I think working from home is great. Especially when you're on the road. It's very hard to go back to a normal life after that. I'm trying to establish a base here in Portugal. But it's different and it's difficult for various reasons. I don't speak the language, my age, I'm 38, so lots of people

> in my age bracket have kids. So, it's not the same as being in your twenties with people who want to socialize and have fun and get to know each other.

Another American nomad, Christine, had settled down since we conducted the interview. She had met a partner and then the pandemic shut things down even further:

> Since we spoke, I've become much less nomadic, especially since the pandemic. I met someone unexpectedly in Portland, and we hit it off so well that we've been living together for nearly two years. I still travel when I can (although not this year from COVID-19), but the past two years I still go to the UK for a month in the summer, and I also went to Paris, Iceland, and Disneyland. It has impacted travel completely. I've barely left the house in 125 days, only for groceries or a (masked) walk. Otherwise, it hasn't affected me as much as some. Since I work remotely anyway, I was able to keep working.

Christine shares a similar story as the other digital nomads. Finding a partner made the continued travel no longer an option, and she has been settled for over two years. The pandemic simply solidified her already settled nature of being back in her home country. She has not lost her interest in travel entirely but seeks more balance. This is a story from the nomads who did update their story with me three years after our original interview and during the pandemic of 2020. I hypothesize that digital nomadism is quite exhausting and, therefore, very enjoyable for millennial age folks, but later on, one does long for a place of one's own and more balance. American lawyer Alexis has had great fluctuations in her law career, from making six figures to making nothing, and traveling between the United States and Hong Kong for years. She updates me:

> I now have an apartment in Miami, FL. Before, for 3 years, I was using my parents' house as a digital nomad "blasting off" pad. I realized I needed my own space. I wanted four walls to hang my own art. I also did some more harder-core digital nomading throughout Mexico for several weeks. What I found was that while I was used to taking 3–4 weeks at a time to travel through a city I knew well (like Hong Kong, where I had lived for several years), digital nomading in an entirely new environment where I did not speak the dominant language was a lot of cognitive labor. Add to that a demanding job. I loved living in Mexico City (and I spent a week in Oaxaca, too), but I do not speak Spanish and it was a ton of mental labor to always be reverting to Google Translate. Living out of a combination of Airbnb and my parents' house started to feel very unsettled and unsettling. I travel a lot less. For my job as Head of Operations for a boutique recruiting agency focusing on

> US-to-Asia placements of executives and lawyers, I usually travel to Asia for a total of 6–8 weeks out of each year. Not happening now. I'm 100% remote, but I'm no longer as nomadic. Also, I live in Miami, which is a current COVID-19 hotspot. I can't really ethically travel anywhere even though I rarely leave my apartment. I will say that being a digital nomad – or even just a remote worker – has helped me adapt to COVID-19 remote life. I'm very accustomed to keeping in touch with friends and loved ones digitally. I've been doing Skype dates with friends – bottle of wine in hand – since 2009 when I was an expat in HK. So, bringing these videocall "dates" back via Zoom was nostalgic, not novel.

The nomads' remote work lifestyle blended seamlessly with the pandemic lockdown, and they did not have the negative adjustment period that others transitioning from an office to remote work may have had. This was the impetus for many to take a break from the lifestyle and reorient themselves. Many felt that they did not want to give up travel completely, but they were seeking more balance in travel and having a home base.

Slow Travel

Over-tourism is the rate where certain attractive tourist destinations began to attract far more travelers than they could accommodate, causing prices to rise and discomfort placed upon the local population (Prados, 2020). That was the situation before the pandemic, with tourist hot spots crowded beyond capacity. During the pandemic, images of usually overwhelmed tourist hot spots left vacant filled the news stories. This provides an opportunity for digital nomads and tourists to reconsider local, domestic, and slow travel alternatives. Sally Pryor (2020) interviewed nomads for an Australian news story on how the pandemic was impacting Australian nomads. Pryor finds:

> "Twelve months ago, I gave myself a good talking to, and said I actually really want to explore and spend more time doing some really deep meaningful travel in Australia, rather than going abroad," Caro Ryan says. "Rather than just a couple of days in each place, I want to spend a couple of weeks to really get into a town or a local region, and COVID-19 has kind of forced that upon us." She's noticed a huge spike in interest in Australian travel from her large online readership and sees changes in the water for the local travel industry. That said, he's anxious to point out that, after decades of extreme levels of travelling, he's really toned it down. Having made a "last-minute" dash to Nepal to go hiking in January, David McGonigal's only really had to cancel three trips in the interim – to Madagascar, Bali and Las Vegas. Meanwhile, the travel-writing community, he says, has now had to take a collective breath and rethink the future. "There's disruption everywhere,

> and it's kind of a chance to step back and say, what do I want to do?" he says … With magazines going out of print, and travel agencies on hiatus the world over, McGonigal had plans to write a book during lockdown in Australia … But like Ryan and Croke, he sees a bright spot in all the halted chaos, and that's the chance that more people, himself included, might choose instead to travel around Australia.

Traveling around one's native Australia can create a new sense of pride and connection with one's home country and contribute to its economy. Scottish nomad Jemma had traveled with her boyfriend for years as a nomad couple. When she updated me on her current pandemic pause, she shared that her relationship had ended, but she now travels with other women, some of whom she met at the retreat we attended together, and she rotates around bases she has created around her family and friends. Therefore, she is connected to and a part of her community and contributes to it with her sustained presence. Jemma states:

> My relationship with my partner broke down at the end of 2018. I started to travel more with other female digital nomads in friendship groups, as well as travelling solo. For example, I spent a month in Croatia with Carole, Meredith and Marcella (who were also at the retreat). I've also become more involved in the expat group Girl Gone International. My travel style was always slow, spending months at a time in a place, and in 2019 I split most of my time between Edinburgh (Scotland) where I have a home base, The Algarve (Portugal) where my dad lives and Berlin where I have a large friend group.

For Taylor, the American expat in Guatemala, she didn't share the issues of loneliness and burnout common to most nomads, perhaps because of her practice of slow travel. She states:

> People say that you'll get burnt out at some point. But I don't travel too much, just once every 3 months. Being in Central America is so grounding. I live in Guatemala most of the time. Having a home to me is just not on my radar. As long as I keep traveling as slowly as I do, I think I'll be able to keep this up for a very long time.

She is a part of her local community in Antigua, Guatemala, home to a blend of expats and locals, Spanish speakers, and indigenous people. She has put the effort into learning Spanish, and she had demonstrated her long-term commitment, by volunteering in the summer camp and embedding in the village. She is one of the few nomads who actually spoke of the local people and culture as a reason for staying. Often, nomads only speak of things such as affordability, good weather, beautiful landscape, but their description of place are generic, disconnected from the actual individuality of the country in which they find themselves located. Locals can tell that such travelers have no genuine interest in their country, and this can breed further resentment. Indeed, Putra and Agirachman (2016) argue that such slow travel is crucial if one truly wants to connect with locals:

> Whereas tourism often identified with short trip, creative tourism in its relation to coworking space requires nomads to spend a considerable amount of time to understand and involve in the local life. Slow tourism can correctly address this issue, discovery, learning, and sharing is the main issue instead of objectified experience. Slowing the pace of travel also provides opportunities to interact and connect with local people and places on a deeper level. (p. 175)

Downshifting

In his book *Growing Up Absurd*, Paul Goodman (1956) posits his primary question: "Socialization to what? To what dominant society and available culture?" (p. 11). There are always subcultures that challenge the dominant culture in their own particular way. Goodman is a utopian writer publishing before the cultural revolution of the 1960s and 1970s, which brought to the foreground counterculture movements. Bookchin (1971) states: "Dropping out" becomes a mode of dropping in-into the tentative, experimental, and as yet highly ambiguous, social relations of utopia (p. 16). While digital nomads question some aspects of mainstream culture – the centrality of work over leisure and experience – they reinforce other dominant paradigms, such as their pro-capitalist, anti-tax, and neoliberal mindset. Illich (1973) states "the higher we are on the pyramid, the less likely we are to give up time to simple idleness and to apparently nonproductive pursuits" (p. 80). Digital nomads trade in one set of distinction for another. They compete in the realm of travel and leisure – prominently posting the numbers of countries one's visited, creating the most glamorous and processed images of a selfie in paradise, and writing pithy statements, but nothing too heavy. Gaining followers and then monetizing one's account is the goals. Performing the best curated photos of one's projected life becomes a potential revenue stream. But, Illich points out, this is little improvement, as "almost everyone in rich societies is a destructive consumer" (p. 102). One is simply admitting one's culpability to planetary destruction. Illich foresaw the fallout of the pandemic in his statement "almost overnight people will lose confidence not only in the major institutions but also in the miracle prescriptions of the world-be crisis managers" (p. 103). Joining the dominant culture surely reinforces pathways of power, finance, and dominance. But dropping out to a Western life of leisure also wreaks environmental havoc. Some nomads and travelers are promoting what they have labeled "slow travel," "downshifting," or "slow living":

> In essence slow living could be described as a life that is outwardly simple and inwardly rich. The interpretation of "slow" therefore

> in this sense is a lifestyle choice and could be linked to the concepts of voluntary simplicity and downshifting as a way of seeking a more meaningful and balanced life. We explore the concept of "slow" and its relation to leisure with a particular focus towards holidaymaking and the development of the terms, slow travel and slow tourism. (p. 19)

Henderson (2014) elaborates on how downshifters may spend their time that they have gained by opting out of the corporate workforce:

> [...] voluntary simplicity as a sustainable way of living ... Example might include spending more time with family and friends, time in nature and involvement in non-consumptive (e.g., non-motorized) outdoor activities biking or taking public transportation, exercising, playing music, becoming more self-reliant (e.g., gardening and making gifts), reading, buying used equipment instead of the newest gear or leisure gadgets, and community volunteering. (p. 74)

Hamilton and Mail (2003) point out that rather than the image of the societal dropout, a downshifter has made a very conscious effort and perhaps given up a prestigious job in exchange for more personal time. It's an investment in a different pathway and lifestyle. Hamilton and Mail (2003) write:

> Downshifters display an unusual degree of resolve as they have made a conscious decision to resist powerful social pressures to pursue the norms of success defined by consumer society. The decision to downshift is all the more difficult because of the absence of everyday role models. (p. 39)

Environmental Impacts

Historically, the United States was the most culpable carbon emitter globally, but it has since been overtaken by China, who is now is first place for CO_2 emissions, with a 54.6% increase since the 2005 Kyoto Protocol (Rapier, 2019). India is in third place, with a 105.8% rise in emissions since 2005; although half the global output of the United States – and the per capita rate is highest in the United States, with China at half the rate, and India, far lower (Rapier, 2019). And according to *Nature*, global tourism is responsible for 8% of global greenhouse gas emissions, with transportation, shopping, and food being significant contributors (Lenzen et al., 2018). However, the mentality of Western high-carbon emitting populations remains wedded to overconsumption without concern. When teenage Swedish activist Greta Thunberg sailed to the United States to attend the United Nations Climate Action Summit in 2019, continuing her boycott of airplane travel, the majority of social media responses to her action were critical and dismissive, with only 30% expressing inspiration (Mkono, Hughes, & Echentille, 2020). As digital nomads are primarily from high-carbon emitting countries, they take for granted their ability for endless and affordable travel, and they contribute highly to carbon emissions. Nomadic Matt (2020) addressed the environmental impact of travel in this post-pandemic landscape:

> Everyone can literally start from zero to create a more sustainable travel sector. Will this mean it will be as easy to travel in the future as it was in the past? Maybe. Maybe not. We should spread out our tourism more. Iceland is more than Reykjavik and the Blue Lagoon. Spain is more than Madrid and Barcelona. Venice isn't big enough to handle all our numbers. Indonesia has over seventeen thousand islands. It's not just Bali. That might raise prices for some destinations but long before this boom in travel, there was budget travel. There have always been ways to save money on the road. There will still be ways to save money on the road when this is all over. I'm not worried about travel becoming too expensive. Even if some places become less accessible (and, honestly, to protect places like the Galapagos, Everest, or the Machu Picchu, we *should* greatly reduce the numbers who go there), there's still plenty of places in the world on a budget! But that is a problem for later because, as the crowds grow slower than destinations and companies hope, by the time we have a conversation about what "the future" looks like, most travel companies will be out of business anyway. What is coming is a seismic shift as large as when the internet transformed how we book travel and get information. And I don't think we're prepared for that.

Nomadic Matt is far ahead of the pack of nomads posting on YouTube about pandemic travel and their adjustments. Scaling back may infringe upon our desires; but our connections to each other and the global impacts of our actions makes us responsible for this planetary destruction. Americans especially have incredible difficulty in making personal sacrifice for the common good, as our capitalist mentality positions overconsumption as a God-given right. In his article "Our 'pursuit of happiness' is Killing the Planet," James Taub (2020) debates the balance between private pleasures and collective survival. By not coming together as a global community to reduce the wide-ranging outcomes of climate change, few of us will have much of a stable globe to visit in the future. He argues that the sacrifices we make now to ward off the worst outcomes of climate change are going to be a much easier sacrifices, than the unrelenting devastation to come, for so many hundreds of millions of humans.

Travel has a tremendously negative impact on the environment. Sustainable travel is more of a buzzword and marketing device than a reality. A smaller trend is called "regenerative travel," which has the aim of leaving a place better than one found it. Elaine Glusac's (2020) article outlines various organizations working toward this outcome, such as supporting sustainable businesses, creating taxes that fund sustainability projects, and bringing money into local communities that are equipped to foster better outcomes. Some of the organizations work closely with local communities and engage in a dialogue to see exactly how these communities would envision tourism as a boon for their land.

Mass Tourism, Gentrification, and Social Unrest

In Bauman's liquid society, the bonds between people are increasingly tenuous, and this creates a less cohesive society, one in which economic and environmental refugees are shunned and when tourists are better treated than local citizens. Bauman (2004) warns us:

> And where there is no long-term thinking, no expectation of connection, there is hardly a sense of shared destiny, a feeling of brotherhood, an urge to join ranks, stand shoulder to shoulder or march in step. Solidarity has little chance of sprouting and striking roots. Relationships are conspicuous mostly by their frailty and superficiality. (p. 129)

Thus, it is the ideological framework that leads to our current global tourism context – in which tourist dollars become more significant than the lives of local residents. The collected articles in Colomb and Novy (2017) anthology, *Protest and Resistance in the Tourist City*, overviews the local response to over-tourism and its outcomes: the glut of Airbnb rentals, environmental degradation, and gentrification. By 2013, Paris was already attracting nearly 30 million tourists a year (Gravari-Barbas & Jacquot, 2017, p. 32). Hong Kong received 47 million mainland Chinese in 2014 alone (D. Garrett, 2017, p. 109). In Berlin,

> graffiti with slogans like, "no more rolling suitcases" and "tourists f off" became a ubiquitous sight, with fierce debates at community meetings about the conversion of residential apartments into holiday rentals became more frequent. (Novy & Colomb, 2017, p. 1)

Local residents in Lisbon formed a group to resist over-tourism called "People Live Here" (Novy & Colomb, 2017, p. 3). Residents in many global tourist destinations have resisted in a variety of forms including in Prague, Venice, and Barcelona (Arias-Sans & Russo, 2017; Pixová & Sládek, 2017; Vianello, 2017). Citizens have also resisted Olympic bids by their cities, as such projects drain local resources for tourist-oriented infrastructures, rather than contributing to the quality of life for local residents (Lauermann, 2017). Inequalities have grown considerably, and tourism exasperates such developments; it does not reduce inequality nor trickle down. Before the pandemic, international tourists were set to reach 1.4 billion by 2020 (Novy & Colomb, 2017, p. 11). Nearly any location can be coopted for tourist exploit, including the development of favela tourism in Brazil, popularized by movies such as *City of God* (2002) and the trend of "slumsploitation," which attracts thrill-seeking visitors (Broudehoux, 2017). Post-conflict countries have also attempted to reconstruct their priorities outward to attract tourists, as "tourism forms a fundamental component of reconstruction plans in Beirut,

Sarajevo, Kigali, Nicosia, and Cape Town" (Bereskin, 2017, p. 152). McElroy (2020) reports on such a case in Cluj, Romania, where digital nomads have been attracted to the "siliconization" of the location, thus creating a "techno-imperialism" in which the Roma are both Orientalized by the digital nomads, while at the same time they are financially displaced by the influx of Westerners. McElroy (2020) calls this outcome a "double dispossession," and calls for a connected approach which "remains rooted in community organizing and housing justice struggles" (p. 3078).

The Lost Art of Staying Put

Digital nomad Matthew Karsten (2019) calls out his fellow travelers in a blog post titled, "Blissfully Ignorant: Environmental and Social Impacts of Travel." In it, he provides little wiggle room for shrugging off responsibility for such destruction, chastising:

> If I catch you trying to pretend you are somehow better than others due to your so-called green way of life, I'm going to call you on it! Pound for pound (of carbon emissions).

Karsten writes:

> Our personal travel addictions are creating more environmental & social destruction than our friends and family back home who don't travel very much. The fact is, no tourism is truly environmentally or socially responsible. All these places would have been 1000x more eco-friendly if they hadn't been built at all. Someone is profiting from the destruction of the environment, and YOU are helping them. If we were really learning to protect the environment as we traveled, we'd stop traveling. If you really want a gold medal for your responsible travel practices, try traveling the world by bicycle or walking.

Indeed, just as the majority of respondents to Greta Thunberg sea voyage were critical and dismissive, Karsten acknowledged that his post was unlikely to win him many friends. And seeing how digital nomads spend a great deal of time trying to learn how to avoid paying taxes, they are unlikely to take his pound for pound challenge. He does not provide any solutions or easy answers – indeed, he only provides difficult options of biking across the country instead. However, such callouts are essential to challenge the responsibility of tourism, as we consider how the most magical and fragile environmental creations, such as coral reefs, or the Galapagos Islands, are set to be ruined by tourism. Thus, more reason for digital nomads to take a moment of extended stay to consider their impact on the environment, local populations, their own human connections, and self-care. British Kathleen reflects on the pandemic pause and how it has provided her more reflexive time:

> And in terms of traditional nomad lifestyle, I don't think anyone's a traditional nomad right now. I think that lifestyle has been put on hold for most people. No one is able to travel. Everyone is locked down in their respective countries. The lifestyle of working remotely has been improved. However, the nomadic part has been stunted. And I'm worried that a lot of the co-working and co-living spaces will get shut down for good.

She continues:

> The lockdown has been really good, in the sense that it's given me time to address the traumas that I've been running away from as a digital nomad. I had an extremely big falling out with my family before I left. It was to do with my mum's care, because she requires care. And it was to do with inheritance, and my sister trying to take all the inheritance, even though my parents are still alive. It was very complicated. During the time of being a digital nomad, I was very upset and angry at my family. That seeped into my other relationships. The lockdown has been great because it forced me to recognize those issues. I was able to really transform, and work on it. And it no longer has a hold over me. There is something valuable to be found in being still. You have to face your demons. Everyone's got them, not just digital nomads. Everyone escapes their problem through drink, or drugs, or whatever, tv, or food. This was an empowering time for me. Maybe not in terms of my career. Because that's been put on hold. I haven't worked, or had income, for quite a while now. It's been ten months since I've been living on my savings. When the pandemic does end, I might do a little bit of dipping into the digital nomad lifestyle a bit if I get restless. It's good for a certain amount of time. Then people evolve, move on, and want something more substantial, more fulfilling in life.

Kathleen had personal issues to resolve but found herself traveling so much she had little time to reflect, until the pandemic. This is when she realized that the space and solitude could provide a healing environment.

In Ellmann's (2017) article, "The Lost Art of Staying Put: On Travel and It's Discontents," she calls us out on our carbon addiction. Ellmann (2017) dismisses eco-tourism:

> Eco-tourism is a nebulous concept, whereby the deteriorating environment is further eroded, so that people who really understand nature can go enjoy its last gasps by surfing it, scuba-diving it, climbing, caressing, coddling, or cruising it. The world's tiniest begonia, newly discovered in Peru, is now at risk of being squished by amateur botanists stampeding up the hill to see it, selfie cameras aloft. Or there's a minefield of alternative health tourism,

> ashrams, hot spring spas to spar in, and ley lines to lie on, a million curative spots that are supposed to heal you in some vague way – but making sick people feel almost duty-bound to go and soak up whatever's on offer, whether it's in Lourdes, Baden Baden, the Grand Canyon, the Dead Sea, or the Alps, is one hell of a despicable idea. (p. 165)

Consumer society has adopted the messages of positivity and indulgence with our orientation toward our own consumption-based happiness over all other concerns. "Do what makes you happy," "you deserve it," and "gratitude (for consumption)" are simply marketing ploys to assuage guilt over the burning of the planet for the making of plastic widgets that will remain on earth far longer than we will. Being a responsible citizen entails an understanding of one's impact upon the world. Ellmann (2017) offers a suggestion:

> What we need is an intervention. Either put these wander-losers on a low-mileage diet or make them go cold turkey. If they need support, they can join Carboniferous Anonymous, a 12-step program for fossil fuel addiction. First step, instead of getting god, as most AA people seem to do, recovering carbon addicts will be steered toward nature. (At home. It's right outside the door, if not inside.) Nature is clearly what everybody originally worshipped anyway. We experimented with other objects of veneration, all dead ends. We tied ourselves in theological knots. (p. 167)

On the Road Again

As with addictive behavior, we fail in our attempt to quit. It takes many efforts and attempts before one modifies one's behavior. While some countries are more financially buffered to weather the crashed economy during the pandemic outbreak, other nations, heavily reliant on tourism, will have no choice but to open their doors. As the United States faired so poorly in the pandemic response, Americans were especially denied entry into the majority of countries while the ongoing rates of COVID-19 continued to be significant. This was a new experience for American passport holders, used to visa-free entry to so much of the world. Travel magazines published articles about the countries that continued to allow Americans – albeit with a recent COVID-19 test – not an easy ask, considering the lack of testing capabilities in the country. By September 2020, the list includes 28 countries, primarily in the Caribbean and Eastern Europe (Fox, 2020). A select few countries were offering long-term digital nomad style visas for remote workers – Barbados, Bermuda, and Estonia (Suri, 2020). Finally, in the spirit of slow moving, Deverell (2019) points out that one can leave one's country and also stay put, by becoming an "American refugee," which is the title of her book, based on her interviews with former Americans who have gained citizenship in Canada. Deverell (2019) points to the long and constant history of Americans who have moved to Canada, especially during times of political turmoil and unrest.

Conclusion

In this chapter, we examine the ways in which the COVID-19 pandemic of 2020 disrupted work and travel and the implication for this sort of disruption in the future. Office workers across the globe switched to remote work, thus normalizing the ways in which digital nomads work and expanding the reach of it. Now that office workers were working from home, their experience was different, for better and worse. Workers also had their children with them at home and out of school, thus interrupting their workday, especially disadvantaging mothers and primary caretakers. However, it also contributed to more family time and opportunities for self-care, such as taking a walk in the neighborhood. Employers may have been more opening to hiring digital nomads, where they previously would not have tolerated remote workers. Workers may consider relocating to more affordable locations outside of urban megacities and continue their remote work. Governments may need to get more sophisticated at taxes those who work in one location and live in another. During the pandemic, travel was shut down by international border closings. Digital nomads had to either scramble to get to their home country, stay where they were, or quickly determine another location to quarantine during a global pandemic. Wherever they chose, it would become a home base for a while.

There were already countervailing trends in the digital nomad community promoting alternative ideas on travel, and these simply came to the forefront during this disruption. Downshifting is when those with significant job responsibility purposefully reduce their obligations, by working fewer hours, turning down a job, or exiting their high-pressure career track. They then open up their now freer time to invest their energy into other realms of their life, such as their family, friendships, spending time in nature, or simply resting. Others encourage "slow travel," staying in one location for much longer periods of time in order to really get to know a place and its people and take the time to observe daily life. This reduces one's travel consumption of flights, hotels, transportation, and consumption. Over-tourism has become a massive problem, with exponential numbers of tourists descending upon few hot spots, infringing upon the quality of life for the local population. In many of these locations, residents have risen up in protest and organized against mass tourism, which may result in disruptive party atmospheres, such as in Lisbon or Barcelona, gentrification based on rising numbers of short-term Airbnb rentals, and the loss of local culture, as transnational hotels and mega-tourist developments, such as Olympic villages, replace the previous city landmarks. Ellmann (2017) specifically calls for people to stop traveling and "stay put." The high environmental price of travel is something ignored by digital nomads and tourists, who are strongly resistant to owning the consequences of their patterned behavior. Even as the digital nomads, and everyone else, were barred from travel during the pandemic, they longed to travel again, and the companies and tourist-dependent nations were quick to provide incentives to regain the tourist dollars, at whatever cost.

Conclusion

In 1997, Makimoto and Manners first published their prophetic manifesto *Digital Nomad*, which envisioned the potential for the internet to revolutionize work and free computer-based workers from their office locations, so they would be free to travel the world and work from the beach. Nearly 20 years later, a subculture developed that adopted their concept and applied it to their own travel-based lifestyle – the digital nomads. This book has contextualized the digital nomad lifestyle within the neoliberal economic context. This book also uses Bauman's concept of a liquid society to imagine the disruption potential of work norms and of competing social narratives. Promotional literature selling the digital nomad lifestyle emphasizes the so-called freedom for workers, but this obscures the fact that gig work pays far less than the full-time employment with benefits, which it replaces. As the ideal of full employment gives way to the gig economy, in which companies benefit by reduced expenses related to paying office rent, full salaries, benefits, pensions, health insurance, and sick days; such expenses are now taken up by the worker. While digital nomads can theoretically be full-time employees, freelancers, or micro-entrepreneurs, very few of the participants had full-time work with benefits. Most of the participants struggled financially as they attempt to monetize social media accounts, sell Facebook ads, or write website (SEO) content. Full-time employment was often something that the high-skilled computer workers had once had but had subsequently engaged in freelance work, at a reduced income level. None of the nomads were better off financially than they had previously been.

By conducting ethnographic research based on participant observation at digital nomad conferences and retreats in Western Europe, this book is based on the interviews conducted with 38 digital nomads. The second chapter lays out the demographics of the participants in particular to challenge the concept that "anyone can become a digital nomad," which is a line often promoted within the subculture. While digital nomads are often young adults, those from the millennial generation are predominantly included. Millennials are at the beginnings of their careers, with less disposable income, but they still retain high levels of cultural capital. Such privileges include their strong passport citizenship, they are usually white or Asian, of upper-socioeconomic backgrounds with educated parents, they are college graduates, and they have marketable skills. Makimoto and Manners (1997) predicted that nomads would require "strong bank accounts" to

Digital Nomads Living on the Margins:
Remote-Working Laptop Entrepreneurs in the Gig Economy, 119–121

Published under exclusive licence by Emerald Publishing Limited
doi:10.1108/978-1-80071-545-520211010

fund such a lifestyle and they did not envision it for "everyone." They also made the distinction between computer-based tech workers and service workers, who by definition would remain location based (and thus, left behind).

Indeed, the third chapter turns to examine the particular jobs that the participants held. Most had low-level freelance work that they would find on freelance website platforms, where they compete for each gig, or they write SEO website content. Very few were full-time employees with one company, and therefore, they found themselves responsible for all of their business-related expenses. Few of them received any benefits, and they did not fund their own pension accounts, as they had little money to spare. As most of these young adults had not yet married or had children, their family responsibilities were limited. Indeed, it was hypothesized that if they were to have children, then that would likely end their nomadic lifestyle.

The optimism and positivity inherent in the digital nomad promotional literature was traced to the field of PP, in the fourth chapter. This chapter overviews this subfield of psychology to understand how it came about, who the leaders of the field were, the funding sources that were significant contributors to such a development and application to the corporate work world. Such positivity literature has been a big boon to corporate human resources departments, which hand out books by the hundreds, and hire the motivational speakers. Apparently paying such speakers to shift the focus from living wages, to psychological motivation, is a more affordable expense. Barbara Ehrenreich (2009) has been an attentive critic of the field of PP, as she has followed the money to its application in employment conventions, where educated young people are encouraged to spend even more money in their employment search. As digital nomads are often hopeful entrepreneurs, they are heavily invested in self-help books and motivational literature; indeed, Tim Ferriss's book, *The 4-Hour Workweek* has come to be a bible for many. Ehrenreich and other critics bring to light that PP is a major – and politically conservative funded – industry in its own right.

The fifth chapter explores the world of leisure in which digital nomads engage. As they attempt to distinguish themselves from mass tourists, they still end up in beach resort towns, seeking the most affordable lodging. Chiang Mai, Thailand, has the distinct reputation of being ground zero for the digital nomad community. Thailand has long been a popular tourist destination, stemming back to its official R&R designation by American soldiers during the Vietnam War. Many tourist locations have historic ties to colonial travel routes, which have since shifted their economy toward tourism. Chiang Mai is an esteemed location especially for new nomads who are looking to join the lifestyle. While they enjoy finding other travelers and expats to befriend in coworking places and pubs, they rarely have meaningful interactions with the locals, with whom they primarily engage via the service industry. Rarely, if ever, do nomads learn additional languages for leisure. Chapter 6 explores more in depth this community creation in which nomads attract like-minded others with whom to socialize within the boutique co-living and coworking spaces which have sprung up in tourist hot spots.

Because of this selection of picking others like themselves with whom to build a digital nomad community, the participants become overwhelmingly racially white and male dominated. This has led to another layer of boutique conferences, which specifically target these marginalized travelers – women, LGBT folks, and travelers of color. Chapter 7 explores the unique travel challenges that marginalized communities face within the tourism industry. Chapter 8 pushes the bar further to challenge the environmental and social destruction inherent in mass global travel and if there is a less damaging way to explore the world.

This book has attempted to bring a critical light to the subculture of digital nomads. It critiques the notion that everyone can be a nomad by looking at the relative passport advantage that most nomads hold. It digs into the other social privileges that nomads hold. It questions whether digital nomads are actually "crushing it" and earning "six figures," popular buzz words used in the literature. When directly questioned about their actual incomes, most digital nomads are living on extremely thin margins. Constant travel is devastating for the planet, yet such topics are usually not discussed at the conferences and meetups where digital nomads gather. Overall, I aim to shed light on the larger economic, socio-political, and geo-political structures in which the digital nomad subculture is embedded, and the ways in which this subculture reinforces dominant narratives of pro-capitalism, neoliberalism, neocolonialism, and the continued undermining of Keynesian economics.

References

Abramson, A. (2020). 'No lessons have been learned.' Why the trillion-dollar coronavirus bailout benefited the rich. Time, June 18. Retrieved from https://time.com/5845116/coronavirus-bailout-rich-richer/

Alexander, M. J. (2005). Pedagogies of crossing: Mediations on feminism, sexual politics, memory, and the sacred. Durham, NC: Duke University Press.

American Psychological Association. (2008). Reaffirmation of the American Psychological Association position against torture and other cruel, inhuman, or degrading treatment or punishment and its application to individuals defined in the United States code as "Enemy Combatants." Retrieved from https://www.apa.org/about/policy/torture

Anand, P. (2020, June 17). 'They just left us there': Startup remote year strands customers abroad. Retrieved from https://www.msn.com/en-us/money/careersandeducation/they-just-left-us-there-startup-remote-year-strands-customers-abroad/ar-BB15C-qza

Andersen, K. (2017). *Fantasyland: How America went haywire: A 500-year history*. New York, NY: Random House.

Andersen, K. (2020). *Evil geniuses: The unmaking of America: A recent history*. New York, NY: Random House.

Arias-Sans, A., & Russo, A. P. (2017). The right to Gaudi: What can we learn from the communing of Park Guell, Barcelona? In C. Colomb & J. Novy (Eds.), *Protest and resistance in the tourist city* (pp. 247–263). New York, NY: Routledge.

Aroles, J., Granter, E., & de Vaujany, F. X. (2020). 'Becoming mainstream': The professionalization and corporatization of digital nomadism. *New Technology, Work and Employment*, *35*(1), 114–129.

Aronowitz, S., & DiFazio, W. (2010). *The jobless future*. Minneapolis, MN: University of Minnesota Press.

Aronowitz, S., Esposito, D., DiFazio, W., & Yard, M. (1998.) The post-work manifesto. In S. Aronowitz & J. Cutler (Eds.), *Post-work* (pp. 31–80). New York, NY: Routledge.

Arvidsson, A. (2019). *Changemakers: The industrious future of the digital economy*. Meadford, MA: Polity Press.

Atkinson, P., Delamont, S., & Housley, W. (2008). *Contours of culture: Complex ethnography and the ethnography of complexity*. Walnut Creek, CA: Altamira.

Australian Institute of Family Studies. (2017). Births in Australia. Retrieved from https://aifs.gov.au/facts-and-figures/births-in-australia

Aydogdu, F. (2016). Frame of new nomad. Retrieved from http://neonomadproject.com/nomadology-read.html

Azariah, D. R. (2016). The traveler as author: Examining self-presentation and discourse in the (self) published travel blog. *Media, Culture & Society*, *38*(6), 934–945.

Babb, F. E. (2012). Theorizing gender, race, and cultural tourism in Latin America: A view from Peru and Mexico. *Latin American Perspectives*, *39*(6), 36–50.

Bandyopadhyay, R., & Vrushali P. (2017). 'The white woman's burden' – The racialized, gendered politics of volunteer tourism. *An International Journal of Tourism Space, Place and Environment*, *19*(4), 1–13. http://dx.doi.org/10.1080/14616688.2017.1298150

Barabasi, A. L. (2009). *Linked: How everything is connected to everything else and what it means for business, science, and everyday life*. New York, NY: Plume.

Baron, E. (2020). Coronavirus: Twitter tells employees they can work from home 'forever.' The Mercury News, May 12. Retrieved from https://www.mercurynews.com/2020/05/12/coronavirus-twitter-tells-employees-they-can-work-from-home-forever/

Barroso, A., Parker, K., & Bennett, J. (2020, May 30). How millennials approach family life. Retrieved from https://www.pewsocialtrends.org/2020/05/27/as-millennials-near-40-theyre-approaching-family-life-differently-than-previous-generations/

Baudrillard, J. (1994). *The illusion of the end*. Stanford, CA: Stanford University Press.

Baudrillard, J. (2005). *The system of objects*. New York, NY: Verso.

Baudrillard, J. (2007). *The consumer society: Myths and structures*. London: Sage Publications. (Original work published in 2000).

Bauman, Z. (2004/2011). *Wasted lives: Modernity and its outcasts*. Malden, MA: Polity Press.

Bauman, Z. (2007). *Liquid times: Living in an age of uncertainty*. Cambridge: Polity Press.

Bauman, Z. (2012 [2000]). *Liquid Modernity*. Malden, MA: Polity Press.

Bauman, Z. (2012). *Liquid modernity*. Malden, MA: Polity Press. (Original work published in 2000).

Becker, H. S. (1998). *Tricks of the trade: How to think about your research while you're doing it*. Chicago, IL: The University of Chicago Press.

Beery, Z. (2020). When the world shut down, they saw it open. *The New York Times*, August 24. Retrieved from https://www.nytimes.com/2020/08/24/style/disability-accessibility-coronavirus.html

Benjamin, S., Bottone, E., & Lee, M. (2020). Beyond accessibility: Exploring the representation of people with disabilities in tourism promotional materials. *Journal of Sustainable Tourism*, 295–313. https://doi.org/10.1080/09669582.2020.1755295

Berdychevsky, L., Gibson, H. J., & Y. Poria. (2015). Inversions of sexual roles in women's tourist experiences: Mind, body, and language in sexual behavior. *Leisure Studies*, *34*(5), 513–528.

Bereskin, E. (2017). Tourism provision as protest in 'post-conflict' Belfast. In C. Colomb & J. Novy (Eds.), *Protest and resistance in the tourist city* (pp. 152–170). New York, NY: Routledge.

Berlatsky, N. (2020, August 11). Misogyny and sexist violence is the result of male entitlement. Here's why. Retrieved from https://www.nbcnews.com/think/opinion/misogyny-sexist-violence-result-male-entitlement-here-s-why-ncna1236464/

Berman, M. (1981). *All that is solid melts into air: The experience of modernity*. New York, NY: Simon & Schuster.

Bialik, K., & Fry, R. (2019, February 14). Millennial life: How young adulthood today compares with prior generations. Retrieved from https://www.pewsocialtrends.org/essay/millennial-life-how-young-adulthood-today-compares-with-prior-generations/

Bick, A., Blandin, A., & Mertens, K. (2020). Work from home after the Covid-19 outbreak. Retrieved from https://karelmertenscom.files.wordpress.com/2020/06/who_did_work_from_home_.pdf

Blackshaw, T. (2017). *Re-imagining leisure studies*. New York, NY: Routledge.

Blackwell, A. G., & McAfee, M. (2020). Banks should face history and pay reparations. *The New York Times*, June 26. Retrieved from https://www.nytimes.com/2020/06/26/opinion/sunday/banks-reparations-racism-inequality.html

Bloomberg. (2019, November 7). The spectacular rise and fall of WeWork. Retrieved from https://www.bloomberg.com/news/videos/2019-11-07/the-spectacular-rise-and-fall-of-wework-video

Blumer, H. (1969). *Symbolic interactionism: Perspective and method*. Englewood Cliffs, NJ: Prentice Hall, Inc.

Bookchin, M. (1971). *Post-scarcity anarchism*. Berkeley, CA: The Ramparts Press.

Bourdieu, P. (1984). *Distinction: A social critique of the judgment of taste*. Cambridge: Harvard University Press.

Broudehoux, A. M. (2017). Favela tourism: Negotiating visitors, socio-economic benefits, image and representation in pre-Olympics Rio de Janeiro. In C. Colomb & J. Novy (Eds.), *Protest and resistance in the tourist city* (pp. 191–209). New York, NY: Routledge.

Brown, J., Apostolova, V., Barton, C., Bolton, P., Dempsey, N., Harari, D., ... Powell, A. (2017, April 11). Millennials. Briefing Paper Number CBP7946. House of Commons Library, United Kingdom. Retrieved from researchbriefings.files.parliament.uk/.../CBP-7946/CBP-7946.pdf

Bruckmeier, K., & Wigger, B. U. (2014). The effects of tuition fees on transition from high school to university in Germany. *Economics of Education Review, 41*(August), 14–23.

Brundage, V., Jr. (2017). Profile of the labor force by educational attainment. *US Bureau of Labor Statistics*. Retrieved from https://www.bls.gov/spotlight/2017/educational-attainment-of-the-labor-force/pdf/educational-attainment-of-the-labor-force.pdf

Brynjolfsson, E., Horton, J. J., Ozimek, A., Rock, D., Sharma, G., & TuYe, H.-Y. (2020). *CoVid-19 and remote work: An early look at US data*. National Bureau of Economic Research, Working Paper 27344. Retrieved from https://www.nber.org/papers/w27344.pdf

Busch, E., Nash, J., & Bell, B. S. (2011). *Remote work: An examination of current trends and emerging issues*. Ithaca, NY: Center for Advanced Human Resource Studies, Cornell University.

Busk, L. (2016). It's a good life? Adorno and the happiness machine. *Constellations: An International Journal of Critical and Democratic Theory, 23*(4), 523–35.

Cabanas, E., & Illouz, E. (2018). *Manufacturing happy citizens: How the science and industry of happiness control our lives*. Medford, MA: Polity Press.

Campos, J. J. (2003). When the negative becomes positive and the reverse: Comments on Lazarus's critique of positive psychology. *Psychological Inquiry, 14*(2), 110–172.

Carr, A., Ruhanen, L., & Whitford, M. (2016). Indigenous peoples and tourism: The challenges and opportunities for sustainable tourism. *Journal of Sustainable Tourism, 24*(8–9), 1067–1079.

Carroll, A., & Mendos, L. R. (2017). *State sponsored homophobia 2017: A world survey of sexual orientation laws: Criminalisation, protection and recognition*. Geneva: International Lesbian, Gay, Bisexual, Trans and Intersex Association.

Catapano, P., & Garland-Thomson, R. (2019). *About us: Essays from the disability series of the New York Times*. New York, NY: Liveright.

Cederström, C. (2017, February 7). Why we should think critically about positive psychology in our universities. Retrieved from https://www.theguardian.com/commentisfree/2017/feb/07/positive-psychology-universities-buckingham-martin-seligman

Cerchiai, A., & Lieberman, M. (2018, August 9). *This is what it's like to travel with a disability in the united states*. Retrieved from https://thepointsguy.com/guide/traveling-with-a-disability-in-the-united-states/

Chalmers, W. D. (2013). *America's vacation deficit disorder: Who stole your vacation?* Bloomington, IN: iUniverse, Inc.

Chikuta, O., du Plessis, E., & Saayman, M. (2017). Nature-based travel motivations for people with disabilities. *African Journal of Hospitality, Tourism, and Leisure, 6*(1), 1–16.

Cilluffo, A., & Fry, R. (2019, May 29). Gen z, millennials and gen x outvoted older generations in 2018 midterms. Retrieved from https://www.pewresearch.org/fact-tank/2019/05/29/gen-z-millennials-and-gen-x-outvoted-older-generations-in-2018-midterms/

City of God (2002). director Fernando Meirelles.

Clausing, J. (2019, February 7). African-Americans traveling more, but some worried about racial profiling. Retrieved from https://www.travelweekly.com/Travel-News/Travel-Agent-Issues/African-Americans-traveling-more

Cohen, S. A., Duncan, T., & Thulemark, M. (2013). Lifestyle mobilities: The crossroads of travel, leisure and migration. *Mobilities*, *10*(1), 155–172. doi:10.1080/17450101.2013.826481

Cole, S. (2016). A gendered political ecology of tourism and water. In M. Mostafanezhad, R. Norum, E. J. Shelton, & A. Thompson-Carr (Eds.), *Political ecology of tourism: Community, power and the environment* (pp. 31–49). New York, NY: Routledge.

Congressional Budget Office. (2017). Measuring the adequacy of retirement income: A primer. Congress of the United States. Retrieved from https://www.cbo.gov/system/files/115th-congress-2017-2018/reports/53191-retirementadequacy.pdf

Cook, D. (2020). The freedom trap: Digital nomads and the use of disciplining practices to manage work/leisure boundaries. *Information Technology & Tourism*, *22*, 355–390.

Creswell, J. W. (2007). *Qualitative inquiry & research design: Choosing among five approaches*. Thousand Oaks, CA: Sage Publications.

Critical Design Lab. (2020) Mapping access project. Retrieved from https://www.mapping-access.com

Csikszentmihalyi, M. (1975). *Beyond boredom and anxiety: Experiencing flow in work and play*. San Francisco, CA: Jossey-Bass.

Csikszentmihalyi, M. (2003). Legs or wings? A reply to R. S. Lazarus. *Psychological Inquiry*, *14*(2), 113–115.

Csikszentmihalyi, M. (2014). *Flow and the foundations of positive psychology: The collected works of Mihaly Csikszentmihalyi*. Dordrecht: Springer.

Davis, G. F. (2009). *Managed by the markets: How finance reshaped America*. New York, NY: Oxford University Press.

De Stefano, V. (2016). *The rise of the just-in-time workforce: On-demand work, crowd-work and labour protection in the "gig-economy."* ILO Conditions of Work and Employment Series, Working Paper No. 71 (pp. 1–51). ILO, Geneva.

De Tocqueville, A. (2002). *Democracy in America*. Chicago, IL: University of Chicago Press.

Denzin, N. K. (2006). Analytic autoethnography, or déjà vu all over again. *Journal of Contemporary Ethnography*, *35*, 419–428.

Desilver, D. (2018, May 21). U.S. trails most developed countries in voter turnout. *Pew Research Center*. Retrieved from https://www.pewresearch.org/fact-tank/2018/05/21/u-s-voter-turnout-trails-most-developed-countries/

Deverell, R. S. (2019). *American refugees: Turning to Canada for freedom*. Calgary, AB: University of Regina Press.

Dickson, E. J. (2020, March 27). Co-living during COVID-19. Retrieved from https://www.rollingstone.com/culture/culture-features/coliving-covid19-pandemic-coronavirus-haven-ollie-common-972514/

Diener, E. (2003). What is positive about positive psychology: The curmudgeon and Pollyanna. *Psychological Inquiry*, *14*(2), 115–120.

Dillette, A. (2020). Can roots tourism build social justice? A case study of travelers to Ghana provides insight. *The Conversation*, June 23. Retrieved from https://theconversation.com/can-roots-tourism-build-social-justice-a-case-study-of-travellers-to-ghana-provides-insights-140862

Doyle, R., & Conboy, K. (2020). The role of IS in the COVID-19 pandemic: A liquid-modern perspective. *International Journal of Information Management*, *55*, 1–10.

Driebusch, C., Farrell, M., & Lombardo, C. (2020). Airbnb plans to file for IPO in August. *The Wall Street Journal*, August 11. Retrieved from https://www.wsj.com/articles/airbnb-plans-to-file-confidentially-for-ipo-in-august-11597164041?mod=breakingnews

Duffin, E. (2019, November 19). Number of international students studying in the United States in 2018/19, by country of origin. Statista, November 19. Retrieved from https://www.statista.com/statistics/233880/international-students-in-the-us-by-country-of-origin/

Duffy, C. (2020, March 12). Big tech firms ramp up remote working orders to prevent coronavirus spread. Retrieved from https://www.cnn.com/2020/03/10/tech/google-work-from-home-coronavirus/index.html

Duffy, E. B. (2017). *(Not) getting paid to do what you love: Gender, social media, and aspirational work*. New Haven, CT: Yale University Press.

Duneier, M. (2011). How not to lie with ethnography. *Sociological Methodology*, *41*, 1–11.

Dunlop, C. W. (2017, October 5). The success and failure of the coaching industry. Retrieved from https://www.forbes.com/sites/forbescoachescouncil/2017/10/05/the-success-and-failure-of-the-coaching-industry/#4de5f5fa6765

Dunn, R. G. (2008). *Identifying consumption: Subjects and objects in consumer society*. Philadelphia, PA: Temple University Press.

Dysfunctioning Just Fine. (2020, April 17). Disabled digital nomad Ep. 4: What it's like being a nomad during a pandemic. Retrieved from https://www.youtube.com/watch?v=M0edVNijWjk

Eddleston, K. A., & Mulki, J. (2017). Toward understanding remote workers' management of work-family boundaries: The complexity of workplace embeddedness. *Group & Organization Management*, *42*(3), 346–387.

Edokpayi, A. (2020, February 26). Women of color are redefining the culture of remote work. Retrieved from https://glitch.com/glimmer/post/women-of-color-remote-distributed-work

Ehrenreich, B. (1983). *Women in the global factory*. Boston, MA: South End Press.

Ehrenreich, B. (1989). *Fear of falling: The inner life of the middle class*. New York, NY: Twelve Books.

Ehrenreich, B. (1990). *The worst years of our lives: Irreverent notes from a decade of greed*. New York, NY: Pantheon.

Ehrenreich, B. (2001). *Nickle and dimed: On (not) getting by in America*. New York, NY: Picador.

Ehrenreich, B. (2003). *Global woman: Nannies, maids, and sex workers in the new economy*. New York, NY: Holt Paperback.

Ehrenreich, B. (2005). *Bait and switch: The (futile) pursuit of the American dream*. New York, NY: Metropolitan Books.

Ehrenreich, B. (2007, October 22). John Templeton's Universe. Retrieved from https://www.thenation.com/article/archive/john-templetons-universe/

Ehrenreich, B. (2009). *Bright-sided: How positive thinking is undermining America*. New York, NY: Picador.

Ehrenreich, B. (2018). *Natural causes: An epidemic of wellness, the certainty of dying, and killing ourselves to live longer*. New York, NY: Twelve.

Eichstedt, J. L. (2001). Problematic white identities and a search for racial justice. *Sociological Forum*, *16*(3), 445–470.

Ellmann, L. (2017). The lost art of staying put: On travel and its discontents. *The Baffler*, *37*, 158–167.

Eurostat. (2015). *Being young in Europe today*. Luxembourg: Publications Office of the European Union.

Fairhall, L. (2009). The retirement income system (Australia's future tax system review). [PDF file]. Retrieved from https://taxreview.treasury.gov.au/content/submissions/retirement/Fairhall_Lloyd_20090227.pdf

Feher, M. (2018). *Rated agency: Investee politics in a speculative age*. Cambridge, MA: Zone Books.

Fernández-Ríos, R., & Vilariño, M. (2016). Myths of positive psychology: Deceptive maneuvers and pseudoscience. *Papeles del Psicólogo*, *37*(2), 134–142.

Ferriss, T. (2009). *The 4-hour work week: Escape 9-5, live anywhere, and join the new rich*. New York, NY: Harmony.

Ferriss, T. (2009). *The 4-Hour Workweek: Escape 9–5, Live Anywhere, and Join the New Rich*. New York, NY: Harmony Press.

Folkman, S., & Moskowitz, J. T. (2003). Positive psychology from a coping perspective. *Psychological Inquiry*, *14*(2), 120–125.

Fortier, F. (2001). *Virtuality check: Power relations and alternative strategies in the information society*. New York, NY: Verso.
Fox, A. (2020, August 20). Where can Americans travel right now? A country-by-country guide. *Travel+ Leisure*. Retrieved from https://www.travelandleisure.com/travel-news/where-can-americans-travel-right-now-a-country-by-country-guide
Freidus, A. (2017, November 8). Volunteer tourism: What's wrong with it and how it can be changed. *The Conversation*. Retrieved from https://theconversation.com/volunteer-tourism-whats-wrong-with-it-and-how-it-can-be-changed-86701
Friedman, N. L. (1990). Autobiographical sociology. *The American Sociologist, Spring*, 60–66.
Fry, R. (2017, September 6). 5 Facts about millennial households. *Pew Research Center*. Retrieved from https://www.pewresearch.org/fact-tank/2017/09/06/5-facts-about-millennial-households/
Fry, R. (2018). Young adult household economic well-being comparing millennials to earlier generations in the United States. In M. Moos, D. Pfeiffer, & T. Vinodrai (Eds.), *The millennial city: Trends, implications, and prospects for urban planning and policy* (pp. 53–66). New York, NY: Routledge.
Gandini, A. (2015). The rise of coworking spaces: A literature review. *Ephemera: Theory & Politics in Organization*, *15*(1), 193–205.
Gandini, A. (2016a). Digital work: Self-branding and social capital in the freelance knowledge economy. *Marketing Theory*, *16*(1), 123–141.
Gandini, A. (2016b). *The reputation economy: Understanding knowledge work in digital society*. London: Macmillan Publishers.
Garfinkel, H. (1967). *Studies in ethnomethodology*. Englewood Cliffs, NJ: Prentice Hall, Inc.
Garrett, D. (2017). Contesting China's tourism wave: Identity politics, protest and the rise of the Hong Konger city state movement. In C. Colomb & J. Novy (Eds.), *Protest and resistance in the tourist city* (pp. 107–128). New York, NY: Routledge.
Garrett, L. E., Spreitzer, G. M., & Bacevice, P. A. (2017). Co-constructing a sense of community at work: The emergence of community in coworking spaces. *Organizational Studies*, *38*(6), 821–842.
Geiselberger, H. (2017). *The great regression*. New York, NY: Polity. Kindle edition.
Gibson-Graham, J. K. (2014). Rethinking the economy with thick description and weak theory. *Current Anthropology*, *55*(S9), S147–S153.
Gleeson, D., & Erben, M. (1976). Meaning in context: Notes towards a critique of ethnomethodology. *The British Journal of Sociology*, *27*(4), 474–483.
Gmelch, G. (2012). *Behind the smile: The working lives of Caribbean tourism*. Bloomington, IN: Indiana University Press.
Goodman, P. (1956). *Growing up absurd*. New York, NY: Vantage.
Government Equalities Office. (2019). Gender equality monitor. Retrieved from https://assets.publishing.service.gov.uk/government/uploads/system/uploads/attachment_data/file/814080/GEO_GEEE_Strategy_Gender_Equality_Monitor_tagged.pdf
Graeber, D. (2012). *Debt: The first 5,000 years*. Brooklyn, NY: Melville House.
Graeber, D. (2018). *Bullshit jobs: A theory*. New York, NY: Simon & Schuster.
Gravari-Barbas, M., & Jacquot, S. (2017). No conflict? Discourses and management of tourism-related tensions in Paris. In C. Colomb & J. Novy (Eds.), *Protest and resistance in the tourist city* (pp. 31–51). New York, NY: Routledge.
Green, E., & Singelton, C. (2006). Risky bodies at leisure: Young women negotiating space and place. *Sociology*, *40*(5), 853–871.
Green, P. (2020a). Disruptions of self, place and mobility: Digital nomads in Chiang Mai. *Thailand. Mobilities*, *15*(3), 431–445.
Green, P. (2020b). Thinking within, across and beyond lifestyle paradigms: Later-life mobility histories and practices 'in' Ubud, Bali. *Ethnography*, *21*(2), 241–260.

Griffin, G. B. (1998). Speaking of whiteness: Disrupting white innocence. *The Journal of Midwest Modern Language Association, 31*(3), 3–14.

Griffith, E. (2020). The digital nomads did not prepare for this. *The New York Times*, November 8. Retrieved from https://www.nytimes.com/2020/11/08/business/digital-nomads-regret.html

Guignon, C. (2004). *On being authentic*. New York, NY: Routledge.

Haag, M. (2020, May 12). Manhattan faces a reckoning if working from home becomes the norm. Retrieved from https://www.nytimes.com/2020/05/12/nyregion/coronavirus-work-from-home.html

Hackworth, J. (2006). *The neoliberal city: Governance, ideology, and development in American urbanism*. Ithaca, NY: Cornell University Press.

Hagerman, M. A. (2018). *White kids: Growing up with privilege in a racially divided America*. New York, NY: New York University Press.

Hamilton, C., & Mail, E. (2003). Downshifting in Australia: A sea-change in the pursuit of happiness. *The Australia Institute*. Retrieved from http://www.tai.org.au/sites/defualt/files/DP50_8.pdf

Hamrale, A. (2017). *Building access: Universal design and the politics of disability*. Minneapolis, MN: University of Minnesota Press.

Haraway, D. (1991). *Simians, cyborgs, and women: The reinvention of nature*. New York, NY: Routledge.

Harvey, D. (1985). *The urban experience*. Baltimore, MD: Johns Hopkins University Press.

Harvey, J. H., & Pauwels, B. G. (2003). The ironies of positive psychology. *Psychological Inquiry, 14*(2), 125–128.

Haworth, J. (2014). Leisure, life, enjoyment and well-being. In S. Elkington & S. J. Gammon (Eds.), *Contemporary perspectives in leisure: Meanings, motives and lifelong learning* (pp. 39–53). New York, NY: Routledge.

Head, T. (2019). SA's voter turnout "lowest ever": Here's how it compares to other countries. The South African, May 9. Retrieved from https://www.thesouthafrican.com/news/south-africa-elections-2019-latest-voter-turnout-figure/

Heil, M. (2019, May 8). The most important resources of LGBTQ travelers. Retrieved from https://www.afar.com/magazine/the-most-important-resources-for-lgbtq-travelers

Henderson, K. A. (2014). The unsustainability of leisure: The sustainability of just leisure. In S. Elkington & S. J. Gammon (Eds), *Contemporary perspectives in leisure: Meanings, motives and lifelong learning* (pp. 67–78). New York, NY: Routledge.

Higgins, M. (2020, July 23). Where an American passport doesn't work: The world, and Irish pubs. Retrieved from https://www.nytimes.com/2020/07/23/opinion/passport-coronavirus-travel.html

Hinton, T. (2020, March 2). Number of Chinese students in Australia from 2010 to 2019, by educational sector. Statista, March 2. Retrieved from https://www.statista.com/statistics/430276/number-of-chinese-students-in-australia-by-education-sector/

Hiroto, D. S., & Seligman, M. E. P. (1975). Generality of learned helplessness in man. *Journal of Personality and Social Psychology, 31*(2), 311–327. doi:10.1037/h0076270

Hoffower, H. (2019). Millennials only hold 3% of total US wealth, and that's a shockingly small sliver of what baby boomers had at their age. Business Insider, December 5. Retrieved from https://www.businessinsider.com/millennials-less-wealth-net-worth-compared-to-boomers-2019-12

Holder, R. (2020). Soul Society 101. Retrieved from https://www.soulsociety101.com/

Hollingsworth, J., & Kwon, J. (2020). South Korea sees the largest turnout in almost 30 years in election held during coronavirus outbreak. CNN World, April 16. Retrieved from https://www.cnn.com/2020/04/15/asia/south-korea-election-intl-hnk/index.html

Holzman, L. (2013). Critical psychology, philosophy, and social therapy. *Human Studies, 36*(4), 471–489.

Hunter, A. (2015). Crowdfunding independent and freelance journalism: Negotiating journalistic norms of autonomy and objectivity. *New Media & Society*, *17*(2), 272–288. doi:10.1177/1461444814558915

Ikegami, E. (2000). A sociological theory of publics: Identity and culture as emergent properties in networks. *Social Research*, *67*(4), 989–1029.

Illich, I. (1973). *Tools for conviviality*. New York, NY: Harper & Row.

Industry Global News 24. (2020, January 14). Over 85% of solo travelers are women. Retrieved from https://industryglobalnews24.com/over-85-of-solo-travelers-are-women-adventure-travel-reports

Ingram, T. (2018). *Accessibility: Disabled world travels travel tips for people with disabilities*. Chicago, IL: Sovereign Educational Media.

International Labor Organization (ILO). (2013). *Working conditions laws report 2012: A global review*. Geneva: International Labor Office.

Jacoby, S. (2001). Traveling alone, women often feel … alone. *The New York Times*, February 18. Retrieved from https://www.nytimes.com/2001/02/18/travel/traveling-alone-women-often-feel-alone.html?searchResultPosition=3

Jiao, J., & Wegmann, J. (2018). Urban vacation rentals and the housing market: Boon or bane in the millennial city. In M. Moos, D. Pfeiffer, & T. Vinodrai (Eds.), *The millennial city: Trends, implications, and prospects for urban planning and policy* (pp. 224–241). New York, NY: Routledge.

Kaplan, C. (1996). *Questions of travel (post-contemporary interventions)*. Durham, NC: Duke University Press Books. Kindle edition.

Kaplan, C. (2002). Transporting the subject: Technologies of mobility and location in the era of globalization. *PMLA*, *117*(1), 32–42.

Karsten, M. (2019, October 22). Blissfully ignorant: Environmental and social impacts of travel. *Expert VagaBond*. Retrieved from https://expertvagabond.com/environmental-social-impacts-of-travel/

Kelliher, C., & Anderson, D. (2010). Doing more with less? Flexible working practices and the intensification of work. *Human Relations*, *63*(1), 83–106. doi:10.1177/0018726709349199

Kelly, J. (2020, July 22). The rich are getting richer during the pandemic. Retrieved from https://www.forbes.com/sites/jackkelly/2020/07/22/the-rich-are-getting-richer-during-the-pandemic/

Kidwai, F. (2019, January 16). Millennials: China's new economic force. Retrieved from http://www.chinadaily.com.cn/a/201901/16/WS5c3ea92ba3106c65c34e4ca5.html

Klein, N. (2007). *The shock doctrine: The rise of disaster capitalism*. Toronto: Knopf Canada.

Kristjánsson, K. (2013). *Virtues and vices in positive psychology: A philosophical critique*. Cambridge: Cambridge University Press.

Kugel, S. (2011). The gender gap in travel: Myths and revelations. *The New York Times*, September 6. Retrieved from https://frugaltraveler.blogs.nytimes.com/2011/09/06/the-gender-gap-in-travel-myths-and-revelations/

Kushner, S. (2013). The freelance translation machine: Algorithmic culture and the invisible industry. *New Media & Society*, *15*(8), 1241–1258. doi:10.1177/1461444812469597

Lai, T. (2020). Where do digital nomads pay their taxes? Forbes. Retrieved from https://www.forbes.com/sites/timlai/2020/07/30/where-do-digital-nomads-pay-their-taxes/#6099a6462578

Lalvani, P. (2019). *Constructing the (m)other: Narratives of disability, motherhood, and the politics of "normal."* Bern: Peter Lang Publishers.

Lane,L. (2020, June 9). How bad are Covid-19 pandemic effects on Airbnb guests, hosts? *Forbes.com*. https://www.forbes.com/sites/lealane/2020/06/09/how-bad-are-covid-19-pandemic-effects-on-airbnb-guests-hosts/#1f3854d17432

Lansing, P., & de Vries, P. (2007). Sustainable tourism: Ethical alternative or marketing Ploy? *Journal of Business Ethics*, *72*(1), 77–85.

Lauermann, J. (2017). Politics as early as possible: Democratizing the Olympics by contesting Olympic bids. In C. Colomb & J. Novy (Eds.), *Protest and resistance in the tourist city* (pp. 210–226). New York, NY: Routledge.

Lazarus, R. S. (2003). The Lazarus manifest for positive psychology and psychology in general. *Psychological Inquiry*, *14*(2), 173–189.

Lazzarato, M. (2011). *The making of the indebted man*. Los Angeles, CA: Semiotext(e).

Lee, C. (2020, August 25). A wheelchair accessible Ocean City, Maryland travel guide. Retrieved from https://www.curbfreewithcorylee.com/2020/08/25/wheelchair-accessible-ocean-city-maryland/

Lenzen, M., Sun, Y. Y., Faturay, F., Ting, Y. P., Geschke, A., & Malik, A. (2018). The carbon footprint of global tourism. *Nature Climate Change*, *8*, 522–528.

Lewis, A. E. (2004). "What group?" Studying whites and whiteness in the era of "colorblindness." *Sociology Theory*, *22*(4), 623–646.

Lim, J. (2016, October 29). Why China doesn't have a student debt problem. Retrieved from https://www.forbes.com/sites/jlim/2016/08/29/why-china-doesnt-have-a-student-debt-problem/#438410251a58

Livingston, J. (2016). *No more work: Why full employment is a bad idea*. Chapel Hill, NC: The University of North Carolina Press.

Lofland, J., & Lofland, L. H. (1995). *Analyzing social settings: A guide to qualitative observation and analysis*. New York, NY: Wadsworth Publishing Co.

Lucal, B. (1996). Oppression and privilege: Toward a relational conceptualization of race. *Teaching Sociology*, *24*(3), 245–255.

Luczak, R. (2015). *QDA: A queer disability anthology*. New York, NY: Squares & Rebels.

Madison, D. S. (2020). *Critical ethnography: Method, ethics, and performance*. Los Angeles, CA: SAGE.

Makimoto, T., & Manners, D. (1997). *Digital nomad*. London: Wiley.

Mancinelli, F. (2020). Digital nomads: Freedom, responsibility and the neoliberal order. *Information Technology & Tourism*, *22*, 417–437.

Maslow, A. (1943). A theory of human motivation. *Psychological Review*, *50*(4), 370–396.

Matt, N. (2020, June 22). Travel is never going to be the same again. Retrieved from https://www.nomadicmatt.com/travel-blogs/future-of-travel/

Mawhorter, S. L. (2018). Boomers and their boomerang kids: Comparing housing opportunities for baby boomers and millennials in the United States. In M. Moos, D. Pfeiffer, & T. Vinodrai (Eds.), *The millennial city: Trends, implications, and prospects for urban planning and policy* (pp. 198–211). New York, NY: Routledge.

MBO Partners. (2020). Digital nomads: A rising workforce trend. Retrieved from https://www.mbopartners.com/state-of-independence/research-trends-digital-nomads/

McDonald, M., & O'Callaghan, J. (2008). Positive psychology: A Foucauldian critique. *The Humanistic Psychologist*, *36*, 127–142.

McElroy, E. (2020). Digital nomads in siliconizing Cluj: Material and allegorical double dispossession. *Urban Studies*, *57*(15), 3078–3094.

Meng, B., Ryu, H. B., Chua,B.-L., Han,H. (2019). Predictors of intention for continuing volunteer tourism activities among young tourists. *Asia Pacific Journal of Tourism Research*, *25*(3), 261–273.

Miller, A. (2008). A critique of positive psychology – or 'The New Science of Happiness.' *Journal of Philosophy of Education*, *42*(3–4), 591–608.

Miller, C. C. (2020). The office will never be the same. *The New York Times*, August 20. Retrieved from https://www.nytimes.com/2020/08/20/style/office-culture.html

Mkono, M., Hughes, K., & Echentille, S. (2020). Hero or villain? Responses to Greta Thunberg's activism and the implications for travel and tourism. Journal of Sustainable Tourism, *28*(12), 2081–2098.

Mohen, T. (2017). The digital nomad life: Combining work and travel. *The New York Times*, April 3. Retrieved from https://www.nytimes.com/2017/04/03/business/digital-nomads-work-tourism.html

Monroy, C. (2018). Education in Argentina. Retrieved from https://wenr.wes.org/2018/05/education-in-argentina

Moos, M., Pfeiffer,D., & Vinodrai,T. (Eds.). (2018). *The Millennial City: Trends, Implications, and Prospects for Urban Planning and Policy*. New York, NY: Routledge.

Morgan, B. (2019, December 16). 100 Stats on digital transformation and customer experience. Retrieved from https://www.forbes.com/sites/blakemorgan/2019/12/16/100-stats-on-digital-transformation-and-customer-experience/#2230fa6a3bf3

Morris, J. (2020, August 23). Help me build a global database of wheelchair transportation providers. Retrieved from https://wheelchairtravel.org/build-global-database-of-wheelchair-transportation-providers/

Muller, A. (2016). The digital nomad: Buzzword or research category? *Transnational Social Review: A Social Work Journal*, *6*(3), 344–348.

Muller, A. (2016). The digital nomad: Buzzword or research category? *Transnational Social Review: A Social Work Journal*, *6*(3), 344–348.

Munshi, I. (2006). Tourism processes and gender relations: Issues for exploration and intervention. *Economic and Political Weekly*, *41*(42), 4461–4468.

Mzezewa, T., & Moore, L. (2019). Don't succumb to the fear: Women share travel safety tips. *The New York Times*, March 26. Retrieved from https://www.nytimes.com/2019/03/26/travel/safety-tips-female-solo-travel.html

Nakatani, M. (2017). What happened when Japan lowered the minimum voting age? East Asia Forum, October 21. Retrieved from https://www.eastasiaforum.org/2017/10/21/what-happened-when-japan-lowered-the-minimum-voting-age/

Nielsen. (2020a, May 18). Marketers, it's time to engage Asian American consumers. Retrieved from https://www.nielsen.com/us/en/insights/article/2020/marketers-its-time-to-engage-asian-american-consumers/

Nielsen. (2020b, March 2). Wise up to women. Retrieved from https://www.nielsen.com/us/en/insights/article/2020/wise-up-to-women/

Novy, J., & Colomb, C. (2017). Urban tourism and its discontents: An introduction. In C. Colomb & J. Novy (Eds.), *Protest and resistance in the tourist city* (pp. 1–30). New York, NY: Routledge.

Novy, J., & Colomb,C. (2017). Urban tourism and its discontents: An introduction. In C. Colomb & J. Novy (Eds.), *Protest and resistance in the tourist city* (pp. 1–30). New York, NY: Routledge.

Ntarangwi, M. (2010). *Reversed gaze: An African ethnography of American anthropology*. Urbana, IL: University of Illinois Press.

Nunez, V. (2018, April 26). This Latina built a community to encourage other Latinas to travel the world. Retrieved from https://www.forbes.com/sites/viviannunez/2018/04/26/this-latina-built-a-community-to-encourage-other-latinas-to-travel-the-world/#31b419a8481e

O'Toole, L., Schiffman, J. R., & Sullivan, R. (2020). *Gender violence: Interdisciplinary perspectives* (3rd ed.). New York, NY: NYU Press.

OECD Better Life Index Germany. (2018). Retrieved from http://www.oecdbetterlifeindex.org/countries/germany

OECD Better Life Index Germany. (2020). Retrieved from http://www.oecdbetterlifeindex.org/countries/germany/

Open Doors Organization. (2015, July 31). Disability travel generates $17.3 billion in annual spending. Retrieved from https://opendoorsnfp.org/wp-content/uploads/2016/05/ODO-Study-Press-Release-Final.pdf

Pacific Trade Winds. (2019). Costa Rica Education. Retrieved from https://www.entercostarica.com/travel-guide/about-costa-rica/education

Pattullo, P. (2005). *Last resorts: The cost of tourism in the Caribbean*. London: Latin America Bureau.

Pelias, R. J. (2009). Pledging personal allegiance to qualitative inquiry. *International Review of Qualitative Research*, *2*(3), 351–356.

Pereiro, X. (2016). A review of indigenous tourism in Latin America: Reflections on an anthropological study of Guna tourism (Panama). *Journal of Sustainable Tourism*, *24*(8–9). doi:10.1080/09669582.2016.1189924

Peterson, C., & Seligman, M. (2004). *Character strengths and virtues*. Oxford: Oxford University Press.

Pixová, M., & Sládek, J. (2017). Touristification and awakening civil society in post-socialist Prague. In C. Colomb & J. Novy (Eds.), *Protest and resistance in the tourist city* (pp. 73–89). New York, NY: Routledge.

Plecher, H. (2020a, February 25). Costa Rica: Distribution of employment by economic sector from 2009 to 2019. Retrieved from https://www.statista.com/statistics/454908/employment-by-economic-sector-in-costa-rica/

Plecher, H. (2020b). Thailand: Distribution of employment by economic sector from 2009 to 2019. Retrieved from https://www.statista.com/statistics/332341/employment-by-economic-sector-in-thailand/

Poria, Y. (2006). Tourism and spaces of anonymity: An Israeli lesbian woman's travel experience. *Tourism*, *54*(1), 33–42.

Poverty rose to 35.4% in first half of 2019. (2019, March 9). Retrieved from https://www.batimes.com.ar/news/argentina/poverty-rose-to-35-4-percent-in-first-half-of-2019-reports-INDEC.phtml

Prados, T. (2020, June 19). I'm a digital nomad who was travelling the world when the coronavirus pandemic began. Here's why I chose to quarantine in Vietnam instead of the US – And why I'm glad I did. Retrieved from https://www.msn.com/en-sg/news/world/im-a-digital-nomad-who-was-travelling-the-world-when-the-coronavirus-pandemic-began-heres-why-i-chose-to-quarantine-in-vietnam-instead-of-the-us-e2-80-94-and-why-im-glad-i-did/ar-BB15IZd7

Pryor, S. (2020). What does lockdown feel like for professional travelers? *The Canberra Times*, June 6. Retrieved from https://www.canberratimes.com.au/story/6780191/citizens-of-the-world-standing-still/#gsc.tab=0

Puar, J. K. (2002). Circuits of queer mobility: Tourism, travel, and globalization. *GLQ: A Journal of Lesbian and Gay Studies*, *8*(1–2), 101–137.

Putra, G. B., & Agirachman, F. A. (2016, August 4–5). Urban coworking space: Creative tourism in digital nomads perspective. Arte-Polis 6 International Conference, Bandung, Indonesia, PGN. Retrieved from https://www.researchgate.net/publication/316472768_Urban_Coworking_Space_Creative_Tourism_in_Digital_Nomads_Perspective

Pykett, J., & Enright, B. (2016). Geographies of brain culture. *Cultural Geographies*, *23*(1), 51–68.

Qi, C., Karlsson, D., Sallmen, K., & Wyss, R. (2020). Model studies on the COVID-19 pandemic in Sweden, 1–4. https://doi.org/10.13140/RG.2.2.33474.12480

Rao, M., & Donaldson, S. I. (2015). Expanding opportunities for diversity in positive psychology: An examination of gender, race and ethnicity. *Canadian Psychology*, *56*(3), 271–282.

Rapier, R. (2019, December 4). The world's top 10 carbon dioxide emitters. Retrieved from https://www.forbes.com/sites/rrapier/2019/12/04/the-worlds-top-10-carbon-dioxide-emitters/#796c41322d04

Ravenelle, A. J. (2019). *Hustle and gig: Struggling and surviving in the sharing economy*. Oakland, CA: University of California Press.

Rayner, J. (2016). *Generation less: Now Australia is cheating the young*. Carlton: Redback Quarterly.

Reich, R. B. (2013). *Aftershock: The next economy and America's future*. New York, NY: Vintage.

Reichenberger, I. (2017). Digital nomads: A quest for holistic freedom in work and leisure. *Annals of Leisure Research, 21*, 364–380. doi:10.1080/11745398.2017.1358098

Rentschler, R., & Boyle, S. (2019, January 30–February 1). Motivations, mobility, and work practices. The conceptual realities of digital nomads. *Proceedings of the international conference*, Nicosia, Cyprus.

Ritschel, C. (2018). Nearly half of millennials plan to leave job within two years, study finds. Retrieved from https://www.independent.co.uk/life-style/millennials-jobs-career-work-salary-quit-young-people-study-a8361936.html

Ritzer, G. (2012). *The McDonaldization of society*. New York, NY: Sage Publications.

Robertson, P. J. (2018). Positive psychology and career development. *British Journal of Guidance & Counselling, 46*(2), 241–254. https://doi.org/10.1080/03069885.2017.1318433

Rogers, C. (1951). *Client-centered therapy: Its current practice, implications, and theory*. Boston, MA: Houghton Mifflin.

Rogers, C. (1961). *On becoming a person: A therapist's view of psychotherapy*. Boston, MA: Houghton Mifflin.

Rogers, C. (1980). *A way of being*. Boston, MA: Houghton Mifflin.

Rosenblat, A. (2018). *Uberland: How algorithms are rewriting the rules of work*. Oakland, CA: University of California Press.

Rothstein, R. (2018). *The color of law: A forgotten history of how our government segregated America*. New York, NY: Liveright Press.

Roundtree, K. (2002). Goddess pilgrims as tourists: Inscribing the body through sacred travel. *Sociology of Religion, 63*(4), 475–496.

Rumley, J. (2019). Voter turnout in Canada election 2019 takes a slight tumble. Huffpost, October 22. Retrieved from https://www.huffingtonpost.ca/entry/voter-turnout-canada-2019_ca_5daf0070e4b0422422cbe1e1

Sarkar-Basu, P. (2019, September 3). Are digital nomads the harbingers of the future of work? Retrieved from https://www.forbes.com/sites/forbescommunicationscouncil/2019/09/03/are-digital-nomads-the-harbingers-of-the-future-of-work/#1f2661b335b9

Schein, M. (2018, July 5). Positive psychology is garbage (and why you should follow its founder's lead). Retrieved from https://www.forbes.com/sites/michaelschein/2018/07/05/positive-psychology-is-garbage-and-why-you-should-follow-its-founders-lead/#439ebf9271a9

Schlagwein, D., & Jarrahi, M. H. (2020). The mobilities of digital work: The case of digital nomadism. *Twenty*-eight *European* conference on information systems, Marrakesh.

Schor, J. B. (2017). Does the sharing economy increase inequality within the eighty percent? Findings from a qualitative study of platform providers. *Cambridge Journal of Regions, Economy and Society, 10*, 263–279. doi:10.1093/cjres/rsw047

Schor, J. B., & Attwood-Charles, W. (2017). The "sharing" economy: Labor, inequlity, and social connection on for-profit platforms. *Sociology Compass, 11*(8), 1–16. doi:10.1111/soc4.12493

Scott, J. C. (2012). *Two cheers for anarchism: Six easy pieces on autonomy, dignity, and meaningful work and play*. Princeton, NJ: Princeton University Press.

Seligman, M. E. P. (1972). Learned helplessness. *Annual Review of Medicine, 23*(1), 407–412. doi:10.1146/annurev.me.23.020172.002203

Seligman, M. E. P. (1975). *Helplessness: On depression, development, and death*. San Francisco, CA: W. H. Freeman.

Seligman, M. E. P. (2002). *Authentic happiness: Using the new positive psychology to realize your potential for lasting fulfillment*. New York, NY: Free Press.

Seligman, M. E. P. (2010, June 20). A letter to the editor by Martin Seligman. Retrieved from https://www.voltairenet.org/article165964.html

Seligman, M. E. P. (2011). *Flourish: A visionary new understanding of happiness and well-being*. New York, NY: Free Press.

Seligman, M. E. P., & Csikszentmihalyi, M. (2000). Positive psychology. *American Psychologist, 55*(1), 5–14.

Sharma, A. (2020). Airbnb to slash 25% of workforce as coronavirus crisis bites. *N Business*. Retrieved from https://www.thenational.ae/business/economy/airbnb-to-slash-25-of-workforce-as-coronavirus-crisis-bites-1.1015612

Shearmur, R. (2018). The Millennial urban space economy: Dissolving workplaces and the de-localization of economic value-creation. In M. Moos, D. Pfeiffer, & T. Vinodrai (Eds.), *The millennial city: Trends, implications, and prospects for urban planning and policy* (pp. 89–109). New York, NY: Routledge.

Singal, J. (2014, December 9). Meet the psychologists who helped the CIA torture. Retrieved from https://www.thecut.com/2014/12/meet-the-shrinks-who-helped-the-cia-torture.html

Slee, T. (2017). *What's yours is mine: Against the sharing economy*. New York, NY: OR Books.

Solijonov, A. (2016, December 31). Voter turnout trends around the world. *Institute for Democracy and Electoral Assistance*. Retrieved from https://www.idea.int/sites/default/files/publications/voter-turnout-trends-around-the-world.pdf

Solis, M. (2020). Naomi Klein: Coronavirus is the perfect disaster for disaster capitalism. *Migrate: Reader Supported News*, March 14. Retrieved from https://migrate.readersupportednews.org/opinion2/277-75/61852-focus-naomi-klein-coronavirus-is-the-perfect-disaster-for-disaster-capitalism

Sonneland, H. K. (2018, January 18). Explainer: Costa Rica's 2018 Elections. *Americas Society Council of the Americas*. Retrieved from https://www.as-coa.org/articles/explainer-costa-ricas-2018-elections

Specia, M., & Mzezewa, T. (2019). Adventurous. Alone. Attacked. *The New York Times*, March 25. Retrieved from https://www.nytimes.com/2019/03/25/travel/solo-female-travel.html

Spiegel Staff. (2012). Germans fear poverty even after life of work. *Spiegel Online*, September 13. Retrieved from http://www.spiegel.de/international/germany/germans-fear-poverty-in-retirement-even-after-life-of-work-a-855352.html

Spracklen, K. (2013). *Whiteness and leisure*. New York, NY: Palgrave MacMillan.

Stebbins, R. A. (2001). Serious leisure. *Society, May/June*, 53–57.

Stebbins, R. A. (2007). *Serious leisure: A perspective for our time*. New Brunswick, NJ: Transaction Publishers.

Stein, K. (2011). Getting away from it all: The construction and management of temporary identities on Vacation. *Symbolic Interaction, 34*(2), 290–308.

Stein, S. (2019). *Capital city: Gentrification and the real estate state*. New York, NY: Verso.

Strzemien, A., Bennett, J., Ma, T., & Lyons, E. (2020, August 20). Out of office: A survey of our new work lives. Retrieved from https://www.nytimes.com/2020/08/20/style/working-from-home.html

Sundararajan, A. (2016). *The sharing economy: The end of employment and the rise of crowd-based capitalism*. Cambridge, MA: The MIT Press. Kindle book.

Sundararajan, L. (2005). Happiness donut: A Confucian critique of positive psychology. *Journal of Theoretical and Philosophical Psychology, 25*(1), 35–60.

Support Adventure. (2020, April 21). Future of digital nomads: Post coronavirus predictions 2020. Retrieved from https://www.youtube.com/watch?v=wVjahErL7j8

Suri, C. (2020). Why work from home when you can work from Barbados, Bermuda, or … Estonia? *The New York Times*, August 19. Retrieved from https://www.nytimes.com/2020/08/19/travel/remote-worker-visa.html

Taylor, F. F. (1993). *To hell with paradise: A history of the Jamaican tourism industry*. Pittsburgh, PA: University of Pittsburgh Press.

Taylor, J. S. (2001). Dollars are a girl's best friend? Tourists' sexual behavior in the Caribbean. *Sociology*, *35*(3), 749–764.

Taylor, P. (2010). Remote work from the perspective of developed economies: A multicountry synthesis. In J. Messenger & N. Ghosheh (Eds.), *Offshoring and working conditions in remote work*. Geneva: International Labour Office.

Temblador, A. (2018, December 13). Report shows airlines doing little to curb discrimination on flights. Retrieved from https://www.travelpulse.com/news/airlines/report-shows-airlines-doing-little-to-curb-discrimination-on-flights.html

Thailand Household Income per Capita. (2017). Retrieved from https://www.ceicdata.com/en/indicator/thailand/annual-household-income-per-capita

Thakral, S., & Sriring, O. (2018). Thailand plans for even more tourists as numbers top 35 million. Reuters. Retrieved from https://www.reuters.com/article/thailand-tourism-idINKBN1F50CF

The Awkward Traveller. (2019, May 4). 40 Asian travel bloggers to inspire your next vacation. Retrieved from https://www.theawkwardtraveller.com/40-asian-travel-bloggers-to-inspire-your-next-vacation/

The Nation Thailand. (2017, August 15). Millennial impact on residential: How they live. Retrieved from https://www.nationthailand.com/Real_Estate/30323881

Travel Noire. (2020). Join the Travel Noire community. Retrieved from https://app.travelnoire.com/

Uren, A. (2013). The 12m workers who risk retiring on inadequate incomes with middle earners hit hardest by a pensions shock. This Is Money, September 12. Retrieved from http://www.thisismoney.co.uk/money/pensions/article-2418601/12m-working-adults-face-retiring-inadequate-incomes.html

Urry, J., & Larsen, J. (2011). *The tourist gaze 3.0*. London: SAGE Publications Ltd.

US Department of Transportation. (1986). Traveling with a disability. Retrieved from https://www.transportation.gov/individuals/aviation-consumer-protection/traveling-disability

Vaneigem, R. (2001). *The revolution of everyday life*. London: Rebel Press. (Original published in 1967).

Vianello, M. (2017). The No Grandi Navi campaign: Protests against cruise tourism in Venice. In C. Colomb & J. Novy (Eds.), *Protest and resistance in the tourist city* (pp. 171–190). New York, NY: Routledge.

Vinodrai, T. (2018). Planning for "cool": Millennials and the innovation economy of cities. In M. Moos, D. Pfeiffer, & T. Vinodrai (Eds.), *The millennial city: Trends, implications, and prospects for urban planning and policy* (pp. 45–51). New York, NY: Routledge.

Walks, A., Simone, D., & Hawes, E. (2018). Underwater generation? Debt and wealth among millennials. In M. Moos, D. Pfeiffer, & T. Vinodrai (Eds.), *The millennial city: Trends, implications, and prospects for urban planning and policy* (pp. 67–87). New York, NY: Routledge.

Wandering Ravens. (2020). What it's like living as a digital nomad during a pandemic|status update for our YouTube family. [Video file]. Retrieved from https://www.youtube.com/watch?v=ajs9zAT0WW4

Wang, B., Schlagwein, D., Cecez-Keemanovic, D., & Cahalane, M. (2019). Digital nomadism and the market economy: Resistance and compliance. *40h International conference on information systems*, Munich.

Wasik, J. F. (2009). *The cul-de-sac syndrome: Turning around the unsustainable American dream*. New York, NY: Bloomberg.

Williams, T. (2016). Half of Costa Rica "millennials" lack higher education, earn ¢400,000 per month. The Costa Rica Star, March 8. Retrieved from https://news.co.cr/half-of-costa-rica-millennials-lack-higher-education-earn-%C2%A2400000-per-month/45322/

Winkler, A. (2014). Corporations are people, and they have more rights than you. Huffpost, June 30. Retrieved from https://www.huffpost.com/entry/corporations-are-people-a_b_5543833

Wong, A. (2020). *Disability visibility: First-person stories from the twenty-first century*. New York, NY: Vintage.

Wong, P. T. P., & Roy, S. (2017). Critique of positive psychology and positive interventions. In N. J. L. Brown, T. Lomas, & F. J. Eiroa-Orosa (Eds.), *The Routledge international handbook of critical positive psychology*. London: Routledge.

Wood, M. (2005). Nomad aesthetics and the global knowledge economy. *Journal of Critical Postmodern Organization Science*, *3*(¾), A50–A64.

Woodcock, G. (1962). *Anarchism: A history of libertarian ideas and movements*. New York, NY: Meridian Books.

World Happiness Report. (2020). Retrieved from https://worldhappiness.report/ed/2020/

Worth, N. (2018). The privilege of a parental safety net: Millennials and the intergenerational transfer of wealth and resources. In M. Moos, D. Pfeiffer, & T. Vinodrai (Eds.), *The millennial city: Trends, implications, and prospects for urban planning and policy* (pp. 110–127). New York, NY: Routledge.

Wright, S., & Koslowski, M. (2019, May 31). Voter turnout at record low after young people disengage. The Sydney Morning Herald. Retrieved from https://www.smh.com.au/federal-election-2019/voter-turnout-at-record-low-after-young-people-disengage-20190530-p51sol.html

Yen, J. (2010). Authorizing happiness: Rhetorical demarcation of science and society in historical narratives of positive psychology. *Journal of Theoretical and Philosophical Psychology*, *30*(2), 67–78.

Ypeij, A. (2012). The intersection of gender and ethnic identities in the Cuzco-Machu Picchu tourism industry Sacamefotos, tour guides, and women weavers. *Latin American Perspectives*, *39*(6), 17–35.

Zukin, S. (2014). *Loft living: Culture and capital in urban change*. New Brunswick, NJ: Rutgers University Press.

Index

Printed and bound by CPI Group (UK) Ltd, Croydon, CR0 4YY

13/09/2026

14961061-0006